A BOOKLET
OF COMFORT FOR THE SICK, &
ON THE CHRISTIAN KNIGHT

A BOOKLET
OF COMFORT FOR THE SICK, &
ON THE CHRISTIAN KNIGHT

by

JOHANN SPANGENBERG
1548

TRANSLATED, EDITED AND INTRODUCED

by

ROBERT KOLB

German Text and English Translation of

Ein new Trost Bu[e]chlin fur die Krancken
vnd / Vom Christlichen Ritter
by Johannes Spangenberg (1484-1550)

MARQUETTE
UNIVERSITY
PRESS

REFORMATION TEXTS WITH TRANSLATION (1350-1650)
VOLUME 11

KENNETH HAGEN, GENERAL EDITOR

THEOLOGY & PIETY SERIES, VOLUME 4
IAN LEVY, EDITOR

© 2007 Marquette University Press
Milwaukee, Wisconsin 53201-3141
All rights reserved.
www.marquette.edu/mupress/

LIBRARY OF CONGRESS CATALOGING-IN-PUBLICATION DATA

Spangenberg, Johann.
[Ein new Trost Buchlin fur die Krancken. English & German]
A booklet of comfort for the sick, & On the Christian knight / by Johann
Spangenberg ; translated, edited, and introduced by Robert Kolb. — 1st ed.
 p. cm. — (Reformation texts with translation (1350-1650). Theology &
piety series ; v. 4)
 Includes bibliographical references and indexes.
 ISBN 978-0-87462-710-7 (pbk. : alk. paper)
 1. Consolation—Early works to 1800. 2. Conduct of life—Early works to
1800. I. Kolb, Robert, 1941- II. Spangenberg, Johann. Vom Christlichen Ritter. English & German. III. Title. IV. Title: Booklet of comfort for the sick ;
On the Christian knight. V. Title: On the Christian knight.
BV4905.3.S67313 2007
248.8'6—dc22
                                                    2006039578

COVER IMAGE FROM SPENCER MUSEUM OF ART, UNIVERSITY OF KANSAS:
ALBRECHT DÜRER (1471-1528) "KNIGHT, DEATH, AND THE DEVIL" (1513)
GIFT OF THE MAX KADE FOUNDATION

♾ The paper used in this publication meets the minimum requirements of the
American National Standard for Information Sciences—
Permanence of Paper for Printed Library Materials, ANSI Z39.48-1992.

Association of American
University Presses

MARQUETTE UNIVERSITY PRESS
MILWAUKEE

The Association of Jesuit University Presses

TABLE OF CONTENTS

FOREWORD

Reformation Texts With Translation (1350-1650) (RTT) are published by Marquette University Press, Andrew Tallon, Director. RTT are brief theological and religious works from the fourteenth through the seventeenth centuries translated into English usually for the first time.

The purpose is to provide religious works that are not easily available to those students of this period in need of primary sources and in need of maintaining the languages. We thereby seek to keep alive the tradition of *textus minores*. Thus these 'little texts' are not offered as critical editions. To facilitate their use, each text features the original language and English translation on facing pages.

Kenneth Hagen
General Editor

TABLE OF ABBREVIATIONS

Abbreviation	Work
Book of Concord	*The Book of Concord*, ed. Robert Kolb and Timothy J. Wengert (Minneapolis: Fortress, 2000)
BSLK	*Die Bekenntnisschriften der evangelisch-lutherischen Kirche* (Göttingen: Vandenhoeck & Ruprecht, 1930, 1991)
CR	Philip Melanchthon. *Corpus Reformatorum. Opera quae supersunt omnia*, ed. C. G. Bretschneider and H. E. Bindseil (Halle and Braunschweig: Schwetschke, 1834-1860)
LW	Martin Luther, *Luther's Works* (Saint Louis and Philadelphia: Concordia and Fortress, 1958-1986)
TRE	*Theologische Real-Encyklopädie*, ed. Gerhard Krause and Gerhard Müller (Berlin/New York: de Gruyter, 1977-2004)
WA	Martin Luther, *D. Martin Luthers Werke* (Weimar: Böhlau, 1883-1993)

INTRODUCTION

TEACHING PEOPLE HOW TO PRAY AND HOW TO DIE

"**N**ow it has come, praise God, to this: men and women, young and old, know the catechism. They know how to believe, live, pray, suffer, and die."[1] In 1531 Martin Luther, professor of Bible in the new, little University of Wittenberg, at the frontier of German civilization, summed up the result of his reform efforts over a decade and a half. The impact he had made on Western Christendom since the posting of his *Ninety-five Theses on Indulgences* in 1517 may be measured in many ways—political and social changes had been set in motion, a paradigm change in defining central theological questions had begun to reshape learned discussion in many quarters across Europe. Luther himself assessed his impact in terms of popular piety.

Indeed, he became a widely-recognized public figure throughout western and central Europe because he was concerned about the spiritual care of the laity. The *Ninety-five Theses* addressed a problem of pastoral care: they critically examined the use of "indulgences." These ecclesiastical pronouncements, available at Luther's time in the form of papally approved, publicly merchandised printed certificates, were regarded as means to bring about the release of dead souls from suffering in purgatory. Thus, Luther's earliest pronouncements for a wider public had focused on abuses in the way the Church, through its priests and bishops, nurtured the faith of parishioners. Many of his early writings endeavored to bring the comfort and the admonition of the Word of God to the people of the villages and towns, some of whom were literate, a majority of whom could not read and write. Some of them were pious; a majority probably did not take their observation of religion with utmost seriousness. Luther aimed to proclaim and formulate the biblical messages in such a way that both the former and the latter might be brought to trust in Jesus Christ for their salvation, love their neighbors selflessly, and have a sure hope of life forever with God after death.

---

1 "Luther's Warning to His Dear German People," 1531, LW 47:52; WA 30,3:317,32-34.

A crisis of pastoral care gripped Germany at the beginning of the sixteenth century.[2] Old forms of mediating the Christian faith were faltering. For at least two generations reformers of various sorts had been proposing new practices (such as the praying of the rosary) and projecting new perceptions of God's will and his world (such as the "imitation of Christ"). Theologians and priests had circulated their helps for living the God-pleasing life in a variety of forms. Luther grew up in this world, and he grasped a number of the literary media in current use for cultivating devout living. As a late medieval friar and cleric, the Wittenberg professor turned naturally to such literary forms for nurturing his own vision for popular piety. They included meditations on the Psalms,[3] meditation on the passion of Christ, and the "preparation for dying,"[4] along with sermons on the catechism (the medieval program of basic instruction, focused above all on the Lord's Prayer, the Creed, and the Ten Commandments).[5] He also published instructional homilies on the sacraments, one more means by which he strove to strengthen the faith of the populace.[6]

---

2 See Moeller, "Frömmigkeit in Deutschland," 73-85.

3 For example, "The Seven Psalms of Repentance," 1517, WA 1: 154-220. On the development of Luther's publications for the edification of the laity, see Rudolf Mohr, "Erbauungsliteratur III," TRE 10: 51-56, and Elze, "Züge spätmittelalterlicher Frömmigkeit in Luthers Theologie," 381-402.

4 "Two Sermons on the Passion of Christ," 1518, WA 1:335-345; "A Meditation on Christ's Passion," 1519, LW 42:7-14, WA 1:131-142; "A Sermon on Preparing to Die," 1519, LW 42:99-115, WA 1:680-697.

5 "A Sermon on Indulgences and Grace," 1517, WA 1:139-148; "A Short Explanation of the Ten Commandments," 1518, WA 1:247-256; "The Ten Commandments Preached for the People of Wittenberg," 1518, WA 1:394-521; "An Exposition of the Lord's Prayer for Simple Lay People," 1519, WA 2:74-130.

6 "Sermon on Penance," 1518, WA 1:317-324; "Sermon on the Worthy Preparation of the Heart for Receiving the Sacrament of the Eucharist," 1518, WA 1:325-334; "A Short Instruction on How to Confess," 1519, WA 2:57-65; "A Sermon on the Sacrament of Penance," 1519, LW 35:9-22, WA 2:709-723; "A Sermon on the Holy and Blessed Sacrament of Baptism," 1519, LW 35:29-43, WA 2:724-373; "A Sermon on the Blessed and Holy Sacrament of the Holy and True Body of Christ and the Brotherhoods," 1519, LW 35:49-73, WA 2:738-758.

Luther's own writings inspired and supported the work of his students who went forth from Wittenberg to preach. Their preaching brought about deep-seated changes in the perceptions of the world held by the German populace (even though, obviously, as in every age, many remnants of old belief systems remained in their practice of the faith in everyday life, and many remained largely untouched by Luther's way of thinking). Most of these publications were brief and easily consumable by lay readers and those who could not read but heard them read aloud.

Luther did not lead his Reformation alone. He had many helpers and partners who sprang to his side in the first years of his reform efforts. They integrated elements of what they had learned from reading ancient fathers and medieval theologians with their own exegesis of Scripture. Luther's insights and influence, however, shaped the framework for the thinking of many of these followers in critical ways. That becomes clear in their publications. They also shared Luther's commitment to bringing the forgiveness of sins, life, and salvation to common people. They, like their mentor in Wittenberg, had also recognized how to exploit the new technology at their disposal. "Without the printing press the awakening and integrating of an evangelical piety, based on the central idea of the Reformation, would not have been possible."[7] Many of Luther's disciples became popular authors. Among them was a pastor in the Harz mountain town of Nordhausen, Johann Spangenberg. His *Booklet of Comfort for the Sick and on the Christian Knight* enjoyed "an unusually broad circulation."[8] Its sixteen printings between 1542 and

---

7 Schulz, "Gebetsbücher III," TRE 12: 112.

8 Althaus, *Forschungen zur Evangelischen Gebetsliteratur*, 50. Especially with devotional literature of the Reformation period it is difficult to estimate how many editions were printed because these tracts were made for frequent use and apparently were used so much that some editions leave little or even no trace today, see Schulz, "Gebetsbücher III," 12: 112. Spangenberg's tract was published as *Ain new Trostbuchlin/ Mit ainer Christenlichen vnderrichtung/ Wie sich ain Mensch berayten soll/ zu ainem seligen sterben/ inn Fragstuck verfasset* (Augsburg: Valentin Othmar, 1542); *Ein new Trostbüchlin/ Mit einer Christlichen vnterrichung/ Wie sich ein Mensch bereiten sol/ zu einem seligen sterben/ jnn Fragstu[e]cke verfasset* (Wittenberg: Georg Rhau, 1544). Georg Rhau's 1548 edition bore the title *Ein new Trost Bu[e]chlin fur die Krancken/ Vnd Vom Christlichen Ritter.* Spangenberg's treatment of the Christian knight appeared without the *Booklet of Comfort* from the press of Georg Rhau a year before the two works were published together: *Vom Christlichen Ritter Mit*

1597 conveyed essential elements of Luther's as well as Spangenberg's understanding of the Christian life to thousands of readers and those who heard the text read by literate friends or family.

THE REFORMER OF NORDHAUSEN

Johann Spangenberg, born on March 29, 1484, less than five months after Luther, left his native village of Hardegsen for schools in nearby Einbeck and Göttingen at a tender age.[9] By late 1508 he had completed a short period as instructor of the well-respected school at Bad Gandersheim and was traveling to Erfurt to enroll in its university. Luther was teaching there at the time, and the two must have met. Spangenberg entered the circle that had gathered around Conrad Muth, known as Mutianus Rufus, a prominent humanist, who exercised no little influence among the students of the university at that time.[10] Muth belonged to the educational reform movement sometimes labeled "biblical humanism." It sought to restore the study of ancient languages and literature and to foster effective communication skills through the discipline of rhetoric.[11] In this circle Spangenberg probably got acquainted with other future adherents of Luther, including his longtime Wittenberg colleague, Justus Jonas, with whom Spangenberg corresponded and worked together until the end of his life.[12] Other members of the

---

was Feinden er kempffen mus/ Ein kurtzer vnterricht aus der heiligen Schrifft (Wittenberg, 1541).

9 No biography of Johann Spangenberg has been written in nearly three hundred years. Biographical summaries include Jones, "Promissio and Death," 108-136, Koch, Religion in Geschichte und Gegenwart 7: 1536, Tschackert in Allgemeine Deutsche Biographie 35: 43-46, and Kawerau in Real-Encyklopädie für protestantische Theologie und Kirche 18: 563-567. See also Leuckfeld, Verbesserte Historische Nachricht, 110-133. This biographical sketch is taken from Kolb, "Johann Spangenbergs 'Christlicher Ritter'" and is used by permission of the editor.

10   Junghans, Der junge Luther und die Humanisten, 31-49, and Timothy P. Dost, Renaissance Humanism in Support of the Gospel, 72-77, and Leaver, "Luther as Musician," 130-134.

11   Spitz, The Religious Renaissance of the German Humanists, 130-154.

12   See their correspondence in Der Briefwechsel des Justus Jonas, 3-4, 35-36, 43, 47, 48, 93-94, 202-205, 252-254.

informal fraternity included Georg Spalatin, later secretary to Elector Frederick the Wise of Saxony, Justus Menius, later reformer in Eisenach and Gotha, and Johann Lang, later reformer in Erfurt. Not all were present in Erfurt at the same time, but they formed a network which provided mutual support among its scattered members, particularly as they became active in fostering Luther's reform in the places to which they had been called.

Spangenberg's career unfolded in three localities. When his university studies came to an end, probably in the mid 1510s, he became a school rector and then preacher for the counts of Stolberg. In 1524 the free or imperial (self-governing) city of Nordhausen called him as a pastor. The town traced its roots to a fifth-century Roman settlement. It had gained the rights of a "free" city under imperial supervision rather than local lordship in the ninth century. Like surrounding principalities and most north German municipalities, Nordhausen was attracted to Luther's message in the 1520s and sought clergy to introduce his reforms. Spangenberg was among those enlisted. He fostered the reform of the Church, and with it the way of life of the people of the town, according to Luther's model. Furthermore, he was active in reorganizing and strengthening its school system in the two decades of his service there. Though he had rejected earlier calls to serve in other places, Spangenberg moved in 1546 to the nearby county of Mansfeld and assumed the office of superintendent of its churches. The following four years before his death were filled with uncertainty and controversy. In 1546 war broke out between Lutheran princes and Emperor Charles V as the emperor attempted to complete his long-standing plan to eradicate the Lutheran reform movement in his German lands. After Charles' military victory over the forces of the Evangelical Smalcald League in 1547 Spangenberg criticized efforts in electoral Saxony, led by Luther's partner on the Wittenberg faculty, Philip Melanchthon, to work out some compromise with the imperial and Roman Catholic forces within the Empire.[13] Spangenberg's criticism served as a pattern for most of the clergy of Mansfeld, who continued to oppose the Wittenberg faculty on a series of theological issues, casting their lot with the group later dubbed "Gnesio-Lutherans" by scholars. In the midst of the developing crisis after the defeat of the Smalcald League Johann Spangenberg died, on June 13, 1550.

---

13   CR 7:309-310, 313-317, 335-336; 10:46-47.

Spangenberg made his greatest contributions to the spread of Luther's reformation through his publications. It is a commonplace that the Reformation spread because Luther and his colleagues exploited the new medium invented by Johannes Gutenberg. The publication and distribution of Luther's *Ninety-five Theses* constituted the first modern media event. Printers found their new trade the perfect means of communicating the Reformer's ideas to a widespread audience. It is true that the majority of Luther's contemporaries encountered and digested his interpretation of the biblical message by hearing it from their preachers or others who read his tracts in semi-public settings.[14] Nonetheless, they were able to hear this message because it was available in printed works. Even though literacy was limited in the German-speaking lands of the early sixteenth century, literate priests digested newly published books and pamphlets and conveyed their ideas to parishioners from the pulpit. The printed page could be read in informal public settings, in homes or inns, in marketplaces and other spots where people gathered. In this way Luther's ideas quite rapidly reached an audience larger than any commanded so quickly by an intellectual before the advent of Johannes Gutenberg's new medium. By 1520, according to one estimate,[15] Luther had composed some thirty tracts and treatises that sold a total of more than six hundred thousand copies, with a phenomenal impact on the infant industry and culture of printing as well as on Church and university. Both friends and foes alike were compelled to come to terms with his continually developing theology and its implications for the practice of the Christian life.

Like many of Luther's followers, Johann Spangenberg made skillful use of the printing press, employing several forms of writing to get his ideas to the public. He adopted, above all, the favorite catechetical form of questions and answers, which Luther had used in his *Small Catechism*, to treat a number of topics and to support a number of reform measures. Spangenberg's engagement with primary and secondary education in Nordhausen moved him to compose textbooks in basic academic disciplines, including grammar, music, and mathematics.[16] Since teach-

---

14   Edwards, *Printing, Propaganda, and Martin Luther*, 11, 37.

15   Moeller, *Deutschland im Zeitalter der Reformation*, 62. See also Edwards, esp. 14-40.

16   *Bellvm grammaticale* (Wittenberg: Georg Rhau, 1534) (an edition of this work by the Italian humanist Andreas Guarna), *Grammaticae Latinae*

ing the Christian faith was an integral part of public instruction in the sixteenth century, it was natural that Spangenberg also prepared textbooks in that field as well. Luther himself had challenged others to expand on his own catechetical texts, his *Large Catechism* and *Small Catechism*, both issued in 1529, both almost immediately introduced as the basic tool of religious instruction in many churches across Germany and beyond.[17] Spangenberg was the first to take up this challenge. He assured readers that he was not "of the opinion that I could improve on Doctor Luther's hard work, but I want to motivate young Christians to practice [reading] the Holy Scripture, the holy gospel, which is the power of God that saves all who believe. Therefore, I admonish all whom God has appointed to be the heads of households to give their children and servants practice by using these questions and answers every day at the table."[18] In urging this kind of Christian education within the family circle Spangenberg was following Luther's advice.[19]

Spangenberg was not only concerned about the primary education of believers. He himself taught students at the secondary level, and

---

etymologia, in commodum & usum iuuentutis Northvsianae congesta (Wittenberg: Georg Rhau, 1535); *Syntaxis Ioannis Spangenbergii* (Wittenberg: Georg Rhau, 1535); *Prosodia in vsvm ivventvtis Northusianae* (Wittenberg: Georg Rhau, 1535); *Qvaestiones mvsicae in usum scholae Northusianae* (Nuremberg: Johannes Petreius, 1536); *Artificiosae memoriae libellvs, in usum studiosorum collectus* (Leipzig: Michael Blum, 1539); *Compvtvs ecclesiasticvs in pveriles quaestiones redactus, Manu, Scalis, Rotulis & Figuris illustratus, omnibus studiosis vtilis & necessarius* (Wittenberg: Georg Rhau, 1539); *Trivii erotemata. Hoc est, grammaticae. dialecticae. rhetoricae. Quaestiones, Ex doctissimorum nostri seculi virorum libris, in puerorum vsum congestae* (Wittenberg: Georg Rhau, 1542).

17   *Book of Concord*, 349, BSLK 504,35-44.

18   *Der Gros Catechismus vnd Kinder Lere/ D. Mart. Luth. Fur die jungen Christen/ jnn Fragestu[e]cke verfasset* (Wittenberg: Georg Rhau, 1541), *5a-b, edited in *Quellen zur Geschichte des Katechismus-Unterrichts*, 2, , 2. Abt, 299-328. See also Spangenberg's expansion of the *Small Catechism* of Luther: *Des kleinen Catechismi kurtzer begrieff vnd der Haustafel/ wie man sie in der gemeine zu Halle/ fur die kinder handelt* (Halle: 1542), *Quellen* 2,2, 285-299.

19   "The German Mass, 1526," LW 53: 64-67, WA 19: 76,1-78,24. That this model for review of the faith on a regular basis at the daily family meal was presumed, though not always practiced, in the early years of the Reformation is clear from a manuscript by Luther's colleague Nikolaus von Amsdorf; see Kolb, "Parents Should Explain the Sermon."

he recognized the need for materials to help them grow in the faith. Philip Melanchthon had prepared a textbook for students of theology, called Commonplaces [= Topics] of Theology (Loci communes theologici), and Spangenberg provided an introduction to its content for secondary students as well as pastors, again in question and answer form.[20] Spangenberg's literary production also reflects the fact that the Wittenberg Reformation was sung into the minds and hearts of the people. He edited liturgical aids for pastors,[21] wrote, gathered, and published hymns,[22] and also pioneered the genre of sermon helps which took hymns rather than Bible passages as their texts.[23]

It was in the service of his catechumens that Spangenberg adapted Luther's postil form of publishing sermons. The postil, a medieval genre which offered preachers model sermons on the Bible readings for each Sunday and festival of the Church year, became a tool for continuing education of parish pastors in Luther's hands. The pastor of Nordhausen composed questions and answers to help his young pupils review the readings from Scripture which were appointed to be read in Sunday services. His questions guided readers through the content of these Scripture passages with the concepts of the catechism in the background, so that they could learn how to move from the basic instruction of the catechism to the profitable hearing and reading of the Bible.[24] The volumes of this work appeared fifty-six times in print in

20   Margarita theologica, continens praecipvos locos doctrinae christianae, per quaestiones, breuiter & ordine explicatos, omnibus Pastoribus, uerbi preconibus & ecclesiae ministris summe utilis & necessaria (Leipzig: Michael Blum, 1540).

21   Cantiones ecclesiasticae Latinae, dominicis et vestis diebvs in commemoratione Cenae Domini, per totius anni circulum cantandae ... KJrchengesenge Deudsch/ auff die sontage vnd fu[e]rnemliche Feste/ durchs gantze Jar ... (Magdeburg: Michael Lotther, 1545).

22   Alte vnd Newe Geistliche Lieder vnd Lobgesenge/ von der Geburt Christi/ vnsers Herrn/ Fu[e]r die Junge Christen (Erfurt: Melchior Sachssen, 1544); see Wackernagel, Das deutsche Kirchenlied 3: 923-934, and Leaver, "Luther as Musician," 132.

23   Zwo[e]lff Christliche Lobgesenge vnd Leissen/ so man das Jar vber/ jnn der Gemeine Gottes singt/ auffs ku[e]rtzste ausgelegt (Wittenberg: Georg Rhau, 1545).

24   Auslegung der Episteln / so auff die Sontage vom Aduent bis auff Ostern / jnn der Kirchen gelesen werden / fur die jungen Christen / Knaben vnnd Meidlein jnn Fragestu[e]cke verfasset (Magdeburg: Michael Lotther, 1544), with the second

German, sometimes singly, sometimes together (plus fifty-two editions in Plattdeutsch, with seven Latin printings, seven Czech, three Dutch, and one Slovak). This volume of sales suggests that pastors also found these questions and answers good guides for their own preaching.

Spangenberg not only prepared treatments of the pericopes. He was the first to adapt the postil genre to specialized purposes. His *Fifteen Funeral Sermons* took another literary form that Luther had cultivated, the funeral sermon, and moved beyond the publication of a single sermon preached at the burial service of an individual.[25] Those works honored the deceased and provided pious reading for the living, especially the laity. Spangenberg had a different purpose and a specific audience in mind with his postil-like collection. German Reformation scholar Irene Dingel summarizes his message in these sermons: "with a focus on the impossibility of calculating when death might suddenly close in upon a person in view, and acknowledging, as the people of that time saw it, that God can put death to use as a means of disciplne, these sermons admonish [readers] to live a life which takes the Christian hope of the resurrection seriously and to distance themselves from all irresponsible, self-indulgent activity that casts faith to the winds."[26] He prepared this work to give parish pastors a model for preaching on the occasion of the death of a member of the congregation. Thus, he combined Luther's postil with the Wittenberg professor's amplification of the single funeral sermon into a special form of devotional literature in itself.

---

half of the Church year—"*auff die Sontage/ von Ostern bis auffs Aduent*"—attached.

25   On Spangenberg's work, *Funffzehen Leichprediget / So man bey dem Begrebnis der verstorbnen / jnn Christlicher Gemein thun mag. Darneben mehr denn LX. Themata / odder Spru[e]che / aus dem alten Testament. Auff welche man diese Leichpredigt appliciren mo[e]cht* (Wittenberg: Georg Rhau, 1545), see Dingel, "'Recht glauben, Christlich leben, und seliglich sterben,'" and Jones, "Promissio and Death," 166-191. After his father's death his son Cyriakus, also a pastor in Mansfeld county, used notes from Johann's pen to publish two similar works, *Acht vnd zwentzig Leichpredigten zum Begrebnis der verstorbenen/ vnd sonst in allerley anligen ... aus den heiligen Euangelisten Matthaeo. Marco* (Magdeburg: Michael Lotther, 1553), expanded by Cyriakus: *Vier vnd dreissig Leichpredigten/ Aus dem heiligen Euangelisten Lvca. Durch M. Johannem Spangenberg ... vnd M. Cyriacum Spangenberg* (Wittenberg: Georg Rhau's heirs, 1555).

26   Dingel, "'Rechtglauben, Christlich leben, und seliglich sterben,'" 15.

Unlike his funeral sermons, which provided direct models for preaching, Spangenberg's aides for wedding sermons (also a genre he pioneered) reverted to the question and answer form.[27] He prepared similar dialogues between instructor and learner on the book of the Acts of the Apostles and on the topics of secular government and economic life.[28] Alongside his *Booklet of Comfort* translations of two meditations on Psalms by the fifteenth century Italian reformer Jerome Savonarola represent Spangenberg's attempt to cultivate popular piety.[29]

Johann Spangenberg dedicated his life to spreading Luther's message regarding the proper way to live, and his funeral sermons remind readers that a significant part of the art of living well is preparing for death. The treatise translated in this volume reveals precisely how Spangenberg fashioned the vision of life and death he had received from the Wittenberg reformers for the people to whom he ministered.

SPANGENBERG'S "BOOKLET OF COMFORT"

As is the case with the first generation of every movement that sets out to improve society or some aspect of its life, the first generation of Protestant reformers had a wide variety of tasks and developed a wide variety of tools to carry them out. The Wittenberg Reformation placed

---

27   *Des Ehelichen Ordens Spiegel vnd Regel ynn zehen Capittel geteilt/ Darinne man siehet wer den Ehestandt gestifft/ was er sey/ vnnd wie man sich darinne halten sol* (Magdeburg: Michael Lotther, 1545).

28   *Der Apostel Geschichte Kurtze auslegung/ Fur die jungen Christen jnn Frage verfasset* (Wittenberg: Georg Rhau, 1545). *Eine kurtze vnterrichtung von weltlicher Oberkeit vnd Vnterthanen/ wie sie sich Christlich gegen ein ander halten sollen/ aus Gottes worte jnn fragestu[e]ck verfasset* (Leipzig: Michael Blum, 1540); *Eine Christliche vnterrichtung wie man gu[e]ther vnnd reichtumb Christlich gebrauchen mu[e]ge/ beide am leben mit Almosen geben/ mit Keuffen vnnd verkeuffen/ mit Leihen vnd boren Vnnd am sterben mit Testament machen Aus den bu[e]chern Doct. Martini vnd anderer getzogen vnd auffs ku[e]rtzest jnn fragstück verfasset* (Erfurt: Melchior Sachssen, 1540).

29   *Der LXXX. Psalm/ Qui regis Israel intende/ Durch den Christlichen Bruder Hieronymum Sauonarolam prediger ordens/ vom Bapst verbrandt* … (Leipzig: Nicolaus Wolrab, 1542), and *Der lj. Psalm Dauids Misere mei Deus Durch den Christlichen Bruder Hieronymum Sauonarolam prediger ordens* … (Leipzig: Nicolaus Wolrab, and Augsburg: Philipp Ulhart, 1542). Cf. Kolb, "'Saint John Hus' and 'Jerome Savonarola, Confessor of God,'" 411.

highest priority on the nurture of a biblically faithful way of daily living. Spangenberg set himself to this task in most of the publications mentioned above and also in the text translated in this volume. It took form in 1541 and 1542, not long after a devastating fire had claimed almost half of Nordhausen's buildings (1540), a somber reminder of the fragility of life in this world. Two of the booklet's three parts, that using the Christian knight as its image for explicating the daily Christian life and that contrasting Lutheran piety with the medieval piety still very much current in the towns and countryside, were published together in 1541. The next year they were added to a *Booklet of Comfort for the Sick* that Spangenberg composed as an evangelical substitute for the medieval *ars moriendi* (art of dying) literature. He had formulated his thoughts on this theme initially in Latin, in the year of the great fire, 1540.[30] Because the Latin tract is only a "practice run" and also because it does not contain the treatise on repentance or "the Christian Knight" in the German reworking of his thoughts on preparation for dying, the German version is in this volume. Its text is taken from an edition of the *Booklet of Comfort* printed in 1548 in Wittenberg by Georg Rhau. With very few and very minor exceptions it reproduces precisely this printer's 1544 edition and the original edition published in Augsburg in 1542 although under a slightly altered title.[31] Subsequent editions were reset but with no significant revisions or alterations and almost no orthographic variations.[32]

This little volume resembles most of Spangenberg's other works in its use of the question and answer form to make its points. As a classroom teacher as well as a pastor, he was concerned about transmitting not only information but also skills to his pupils in the secondary school which he had revived and reformed in Nordhausen. Modern readers may be surprised that, as he relates in his dedicatory preface, he intended to teach these adolescents how to understand "the art of dying." Two factors made such an effort necessary in his time. First, death struck the young much more often in the sixteenth century than it does in Western countries

---

30 *Hoc libello continentur Infrascripta. Dialogus Christiani & mortis De fatis ineuitabilibus et uario mortalium exitu. Elegia. Origo peccati et mortis. Praeparationes quatuor ad mortem* (Erfurt: Melchior Sachssen, 1540).

31 See note 8 above.

32 Editions appeared in 1546, 1548, 1549 (2), 1551, 1553, 1559, 1563, 1565 (2), 1569, 1574, 1577, and 1597.

at the beginning of the twenty-first century. His pupils had occasion to think seriously about the afterlife because they had experienced the loss of family and friends at a younger age than modern youth typically do. In addition, like medieval works on "the art of dying," Spangenberg's book aimed to prepare its readers to accompany other people who were sick and perhaps dying. The likelihood that their own parents or others in their town or village would need their help in praying as they lay upon their deathbed was clear to the young people of his day. The usefulness of such counsel and training for his contemporaries of all ages made Spangenberg's book popular.

In fashioning his tools for instructing his readers the pastor from Nordhausen was developing not only their knowledge of the biblical narratives and biblical insights into daily living. He was also showing them how to read Scripture on their own. Literature for the laity in every age of the Church's history has sought to nurture personal habits of meditation and devotion. Spangenberg wrote for lay people who were in the first generation in which the new technology of movable type and the translation of Scripture into the vernacular made possible broader use of Scripture in individual households and for personal edification. He strove to cultivate in his readers the capacity to read the Bible themselves and apply it to their own lives. His tasks as a publishing theologian also included teaching them how to pray. This treatise illustrates how this pastor tried to nurture both pious practices.

In general, the Wittenberg reformers strove to bring their people into the framework of a biblical way of thinking. They did not believe the task was so difficult. Heinrich Bornkamm observed that Luther's comment and preaching on the Old Testament was lively and fresh because the world of his childhood and youth in the German village did not differ so greatly from the peasant-like life of the biblical characters. Therefore, Luther found in the biblical narratives a "mirror of everyday life."[33] Spangenberg, like Luther, presumed that the narratives of Scripture and its precepts were immediately understandable to his audience and applicable in his readers' lives. Thus, the way in which Luther and Spangenberg sought to cultivate the Christian life confirms the judgment of American theologian Hans Frei that the pre-critical use of Scripture presupposed that in the Bible readers find the true view of reality that determines how to evaluate the world around them, in contrast to a modern critical view of Scripture, which assumes that the

33   Bornkamm, *Luther and the Old Testament*, 11.

Bible stands under the judgment of the modern interpreter.[34] Therefore, Spangenberg, like Luther, could interpret life around him, and dying as well, with both straightforward use of the observations of the biblical writers and with analogical or allegorical use of, for instance, the exodus narrative or the three biblical mountains of Sinai, Zion, and Tabor. His concern to help the sick and dying understand the faithfulness of the God who had raised Jesus Christ from the dead was easily combined with his desire to help readers and hearers learn how to read the Bible and use its texts in their own lives.

Spangenberg apparently believed firmly that repetition is the mother of learning, for he reiterated certain points with similar questions and answers or with the recurring use of certain Bible texts. Through such repetition and by drawing parallels or symbolic connections between the biblical stories and the readers' own experience, along with direct practical applications of biblical principles to their lives, Spangenberg tried to implant knowledge of biblical stories and biblical teaching in the minds of readers. In this way he hoped to cultivate a way of life and an approach to death that conformed to the biblical vision of life and humanity as he had learned it from Luther.

In that life prayer played an important role. To help pious people learn to pray properly, Spangenberg offered a series of models at the end of his "art of dying." He did not include thanksgiving to God in each prayer even though thanks normally formed one element in Evangelical prayers. Instead, the author focused on asking for God's help on the basis of a clear affirmation of his love for his people and his power over all their enemies. In the face of death readers of the treatise were instructed to use prayer to aid the dying in renouncing the world and refocusing life on their Savior. Simple confessions regarding God's action in Christ on behalf of his people and examples of God's love and support for specific individuals from Scripture delivered the comfort of the gospel promise in these prayers. The texts encouraged both the person praying with the sick and the sick themselves to find hope and assurance in Christ.

As noted above, the text reproduced and translated here consists of three parts. The first is Spangenberg's manual for those who wish to bring the dying the comfort afforded by Christ's death and resurrection. It was also intended to comfort readers who themselves lay on their deathbeds. The second is his admonition to live the life of

---

34   Frei, *The Eclipse of Biblical Narrative,* 1, 3.

the "Christian knight" which resists temptations, depends totally on God, and serves the neighbor. The third is a critique of medieval piety.

SPANGENBERG AND "THE ART OF DYING"

The medieval *ars moriendi* had become an important and widespread devotional aid in the fifteenth century, particularly under the influence of the Parisian theologian Jean Gerson's *Opus tripartitum* and the anonymous *Sancti Anselmi Admonitio*. Both of these works circulated since early in the fifteenth century.[35] They provided aid to parish priests and even to lay people, who in time of plague, when the number of deaths in a locality soared, were called upon to minister to the spiritual needs of the dying. Gerson and his imitators presumed a way of thinking predominant in late medieval German theology based on the axiom that God gives grace to those who do the best they can in cultivating good works. With that grace, based on Christ's life, death, and resurrection, mediated through the sacraments, Christians were believed to be able to earn sufficient merit in God's sight to attain heaven for themselves. Different examples of the *ars moriendi* genre mixed fear of insufficient performance with hope of God's grace in differing combinations. American Reformation historian Austra Reinis demonstrates that the medieval *ars moriendi* operated to a large extent on the principle of uncertainty. Its authors wanted to make sure that sufficient dread in the face of hell and even purgatory stirred the souls of the dying to insure proper pious dispositions in those already in a sickbed and proper pious performance in those not yet at death's door. For already in the fifteenth century the *ars moriendi* gave instruction in "the art of living" as well as "the art of dying."[36]

Luther put his hand to constructing an Evangelical reworking of this genre early on, in 1519. His little book on *Preparation for Death* guided believers on a path out of this life significantly different from most medieval instructions for the dying and those who ministered to them. His teaching on the justification of sinners "brought about pro-

---

35   See Reinis, "Reforming the Art of Dying," 1-22. See also Rudolf, *Ars Moriendi* and Falk, *Die deutschen Sterbebüchlein*.

36   Reinis, "Reforming the Art of Dying," 23-68.

found changes in death culture."[37] He aimed to comfort the dying with
the assurance that God's promise, based on Christ's work, had restored
them to God's favor. He emphasized that when God promises to be
the gracious, forgiving Father of a sinner in the baptismal form of his
Word, he will remain true to his promise. To be sure, in line with his
distinction between law and gospel, Luther proclaimed judgment upon
the baptized who were indulging in sin. He afforded them no word of
gospel and grace. But the repentant could trust without doubt in the
faithfulness of Christ, who had died and risen to bring them to a life
of trust and to the gift of salvation.

Luther's disciples recognized the need for continuing to bring his
consolations to the dying. In addition to a spate of such works in the
1520s,[38] anthologies of materials from the Wittenberg professor's s pen
by others appeared around the time Spangenberg's work was printed.[39]
All these works were designed to assist pastors and lay people in at-
tending to the needs of the dying. They attempted to provide comfort
for those locked in the struggle with death and to cultivate a firm trust
in Christ as well as a confident hope for a life with him forever.

With a series of questions Spangenberg rehearses how the sick and
dying should turn to God with repentant hearts. In so doing his book
offers a guide for the living as well as the dying, as had medieval treatments of the art of dying.[40] Therefore it was natural to attach to it his
program for living the life of repentance, his work on the "Christian
knight."

---

37   Reinis, "Reforming the Art of Dying," 6; cf. her extensive discussion,
69-129, and Werner Goez, "Luthers 'Ein Sermon von der Bereitung zum
Sterben' ...," 114 (97-114). Cf. Rudolf Mohr, "Ars moriendi II," 149-154, Appel, *Anfechtung und Trost*, 105-113, and Jones, "*Promissio* and Death," 1-107.

38   See the overview in Reinis, "Reforming the Art of Dying," 130-389.

39   E.g., *Ein Trost Büchlin fur die Sterbenden. An die hochgebone Fu[e]rstin
/ Fraw Elisabet / Pfaltzgreffin bey Rhein / Hertzogin jnn Beiern / Greffin zu
Veldentz / Landgreffin zu Hessen* (Wittenberg: Georg Rhau, 1542), and *Etliche Trostschrifften vnd predigten / fu[e]r die / so in Todes / vnd ander Not vnd
anfechtung sind* (Wittenberg: Veit Creutzer, 1546).

40   For a good overview of the work, see Reinis, "Reforming the Art of Dying," 69-116, and Jones, "*Promissio* and Death," 137-191.

Spangenberg and the
Image of the Christian Knight

Spangenberg's "Christian Knight" certainly intended to teach "the art
of living," but as readers quickly see, living and dying in the sixteenth-
century imagination were quite intertwined. In taking this image as
his point of orientation for motivating and shaping daily Christian living, Spangenberg was taking a biblical illustration which depicted the
believer as a combatant against God's foes (1 Cor. 10:3, Eph. 6:17, 2
Tim. 2: 3, 1 Thes. 5:8). This metaphor had been employed from time to
time for different purposes in the Christian tradition. Theologians and
preachers in the early Church had described the apostles, missionaries,
all Christian teachers, ascetics, or monks as "soldiers" or "knights" of
Christ. As early as Tertullian (ca. 160-ca.220) the depiction was used
to describe all Christians since their baptisms had enlisted them in
the ranks of their Lord's legions.[41] The use of the metaphor continued
throughout the Middle Ages. For example, Bernhard of Clairvaux had
described the Christian life as the life of a knight in order to encourage
and hearten crusading monks in Palestine in 1135.[42]

Among Spangenberg's contemporaries two leading public figures
in the German Empire had used the theme of the Christian "soldier"
(Latin *miles*) or "knight" (Latin *eques*) to express, each in his own way,
something of the Christian life. The first was Desiderius Erasmus of
Rotterdam, the prince of humanist scholars. In 1503 he had composed
an *Enchiridion* (the Greek word for both a handbook and a dagger used
for self-protection) *of the Christian Soldier*, translated into German also
as *Knight*.[43] This little book sought to give instructions for Christian
living on the basis of the "imitation of Christ" tradition of late medieval

41   See Merzbacher, "Militia Christi," and "Ritter," *Lexikon der christlichen
Ikonographie*, 3, 554-556; and Stolt, *Wortkampf*, 90. This description of the
Christian knight is taken in part from Kolb, "Johann Spangenbergs'Christlicher
Ritter.'"

42   "Ad milites templi, de laude novae militiae," in *Bernhard von Clairvaux,
Sämtliche Werke* 1: 257-326.

43   *Enchiridion militis Christi*, published in English translation in *Erasmus.
Handbook of the Militant Christian*, and *Collected Works of Erasmus, Spiritualia*,
66: 24-127. In the first German translation, by Johannes Adelphus (Basel
1520, printed by Adam Petri) the title was *Enchiridion oder handbuchlin eins
Christlichen vnd ritterlichen lebens* ("Handbook of a Christian and Knightly

piety cultivated by the Brethren of the Common Life and others, particularly in the Netherlands.[44] In this work Erasmus emphasized the practice of virtue without much attention to motivation. Prayer and knowledge were the instruments through which he hoped to cultivate virtuous performance in the readers of his *Enchiridion*. Erasmus's work became quite popular, appearing in forty editions before 1528. In 1520 it appeared for the first time in German translation. Luther himself informed Erasmus that he had read this book.[45]

Erasmus's image of the Christian knight is thought by scholars to have influenced the engraving of the Christian knight pursued by death and the devil that the Nuremberg artist Albrecht Dürer created in 1513.[46] German Reformation historian Bernd Hamm labels the artist's religious orientation "pious humanism" and shows how the poem he composed to accompany his depiction of the Christian knight combined hope in God's grace with a reliance on his conduct of a Christian life and his performance of the good works of repentance. Spangenberg's concept of the Christian knight who fights against death and devil with the Word of God as God's means or instrument of bestowing grace had not yet emerged in Dürer's expression of the faith.[47]

Both these humanists commanded admiration within the Erfurt circle of humanists, and in all likelihood their works found positive reception among its members. Spangenberg was undoubtedly familiar with both Erasmus' book and Dürer's engraving. But the theology he had learned from Wittenberg determined his application of the image. Luther himself had put the military metaphor to use in his polemic; believers must combat every false presentation of God's Word.[48] He had also published a sermon on the passage from Ephesians 6 on the armor of God in 1533, and it is clear that Spangenberg borrowed sentences from that sermon and summarized other passages in describing the

---

Life") but in the second translation, by Leo Jud (Basel 1521, printed by Valentin Curio) the word "combatative" or "soldierly" ("streitbar") replaced "knightly."

44 Post, *The Modern Devotion*, esp. 343-680.

45 WA Br 1:362,19-23 (#163), March 28, 1519.

46 Panofsky, *Albrecht Dürer*, 151-152.

47 Hamm, *Lazarus Spengler*, 91-93, cf. 91-102.

48 Stolt, *Wortkampf*, 95-119.

Christian's armor.[49] This picture of the Christian knight had served other Lutheran formulations on the art of dying as a brief, passing allusion to the nature of the believer's struggle against those foes that undermine faith in Christ.[50] But none of Spangenberg's Evangelical contemporaries had used the image extensively. Nor did he launch a tradition among the authors of Lutheran devotional literature. Although the sense of struggle and confict with sin and evil remained important for their work, his particular metaphor of the soldier or knight never became prominent among them as a helpful portrayal of Christian living.

Spangenberg's treatise reflects his convictions regarding key elements in Luther's theology. The fundamental hermeneutic in the writings of both men was expressed in the distinction between law and gospel. In 1522 the Wittenberg professor compiled his first "Prayerbook," not a collection of prayers as such but rather the raw material for personal devotion, chiefly passages from Scripture.[51] In the preface of this work he set forth a three-part pattern for using God's Word. Sick people need a diagnosis, through God's law, before they will seek a physician. Healing comes in the form of the gospel of forgiveness and life in Christ. This gospel produces a life of prayer and the fulfilling of God's commands, the fruit of the transformation wrought by the gospel. This rhythm of the condemning law and the life-giving gospel, which moved believers to perform good works as fruits of faith, constituted daily Christian life, according to Luther's reading of Scripture.[52]

Both Spangenberg and Luther also presumed that daily Christian life takes place within the eschatological strife between God and Satan. Luther took the person of the devil most seriously: he constantly tempts Christians, the Reformer was convinced, attempting to bring their lives

49   WA 34, II: 360-404, especially 399,3-404,2. The sermon was preached on October 29, 1531 and published two years later.

50   Kaspar Güttel, *Ein tro[e]stliche Sermon: weß sich der Christenmensch hab am todtbette zu halten? vnnd was ym wort Gottes gegründt/ von den sterbenden? Auch waß bawfelligß/ vnd verfüerlichs on den Todten durch menschen leere auffgerichtet sey?* (Zwickau: Jörg Gastell, 1523), A3a, b2b-b3b; Georg Mohr, *Eyn Christliche vormanunge ausz dem Euangelio: Dixit Martha ad Jesum: Wider das zaghafftig erschreckniß des Todes* (Aldenburg: Gabriel Kantz, 1524), A3a.

51   "Personal Prayerbook," 1522, LW 43:11-45, WA 10,II: (331) 375-501.

52   LW 43:13-15, WA 10,II:376,12-377,13.

to ruin, both in relationships with other people, and above all in their relationship of trust and devotion with God. In his hymn "A Mighty Fortress is Our God," Luther described how God's Word comes to give believers "a trustworthy shield and weapon" against "the old evil foe" and "his deep guile and great might."[53] According to the German theologian Hans-Martin Barth, Luther's concept of the Christian life cannot be understood apart from recognizing the role of the devil and his continual assault against God and the people of God.[54] In that regard Barth points out how important the believer's baptism was for equipping the Christian with the hope and assurance needed to withstand Satan's attacks. Such hope and assurance are delivered by God's promise in that sacrament and by God's action of killing and making alive through Christ's death and resurrection in this and other forms of his Word.[55] Early in his career Luther had made this association of the battle against the devil with baptism and daily repentance,[56] and he never ceased to regard his Reformation as the cultivation of such a life of repentance. Spangenberg had absorbed this element of his friend's thought.

Both of them also firmly believed that the best weapon against the deception and murderous designs of the devil was the proper use of God's Word, especially in baptismal form.

Despite God's boundless goodness, the daily Christian life, in Luther's view, still reflects the great mystery of the existence of evil. Particularly critical for him was the mystery of the continued presence of sin and evil in the lives of God's faithful people, to whom he had promised new life in their baptisms. Thus, Luther's conception of proper Christian living, and of the cultivation of his kind of piety, revolved around the ways in which God's Word worked in the believer's life. It was designed to arouse trust in Christ and to motivate good works toward the neighbor. In the Reformer's world most people became Christians through the Word in its baptismal form. Luther used Romans 6:3-11 as a pattern for what happens in daily life, based on the action of the Holy Spirit in this sacrament. There Paul states that God kills sinners as sinners and resurrects them as new people in Christ, so that they can walk in

---

53   LW 53:284-285, WA 35: 455,20-457,12.

54   Barth, *Der Teufel und Jesus Christus*, passim, esp. 11-13, 208-210.

55   Ibid., 171.

56   "The Baptismal Booklet in German," 1523, LW 53: 97-103, WA 12: esp. 44,8-28, 45,20-31, 47,3-48,25.

their Lord's footsteps. Luther's *Small Catechism* had children learn by heart,

> What is the significance of such a baptism with water? It signifies that the old creature in us with all sins and evil desires is to be drowned and die through daily contrition and repentance, and on the other hand that a new person is to come forth and rise up to live before God in righteousness and purity forever. Where is this written? Saint Paul says in Romans 6[:4], "We are buried with Christ through baptism into death, so that, just as Christ was raised from the dead through the glory of the Father, we, too, are to walk in a new life." [57]

This may not be the precise understanding of repentance which caused him to begin the *Ninety-five Theses* with the words, "The whole life of a Christian is a life of repentance."[58] However, in the intervening decade between composing these words and the publication of the *Small Catechism* Luther had come to define the believer's life in terms of the rhythm of daily repetition of this baptismal dying to sin and rising to faithfulness in Jesus Christ. It was this framework for interpreting life that he wanted to nurture through his Reformation.

Spangenberg had learned this lesson well from his mentor. The year before he began work on these devotional tracts he had explained baptism to the readers of his *Theological Pearls* with echoes of Luther's *Small Catechism*: "Baptism signifies repentance and the remission of sins, or as Paul says, rebirth. Immersion signifies that the Old Person dies with sin, and being lifted up out of the water signifies the new person, washed and reconciled to God, Father, Son, and Holy Spirit. For the Father accepts you for the sake of his Son, and he promises you the

---

57   Small Catechism, *Book of Concord*, 360, BSLK 516, 29-517,7. On Luther's view of baptism, see Kolb, "'What Benefit Does the Soul Receive …?'"

58   There he echoed the conviction of the fourteenth-century devotional writer and preacher Heinrich Tauler regarding the continuing necessity of humbling oneself before God; see Leppin, "'Omnem vitam fidelium penitentiam esse voluit.'"

Holy Spirit, by whom your life will be made holy."[59] All this echoed what he had learned from his friend in Wittenberg.[60]

Spangenberg's sketch of this warrior drafted by God through baptism into his company took shape largely on the basis of the apostle Paul's imagery of the armor of the Christian in Ephesians 6:10-17. The nature of that conflict became clear through the analysis of the believer's enemies, the traditional triad of the devil, the world, and self-centered human desires, that is, according to Paul's language, the "flesh." Like Luther, Spangenberg was convinced, that believers had waged a daily battle against the devil, the world, and human "flesh." Since the early Church, Christians had portrayed this trio as the tempters, the foes, against which they must struggle.[61]

That motif introduced Spangenberg's treatment of the life of repentance. He apparently did not feel compelled to remain within the strictures of the imagery he had chosen to begin his treatise. He forged these elements of the "knight" image together with one particular version of another favorite image from medieval piety, that of the pilgrim, the wanderer underway. He selected a biblical rendering of that image, the wandering of the children of Israel out of Egypt through the desert to the Promised Land. His narrative moved to the pilgrimage of Israel through the wilderness so deftly that the reader hardly notices being transported into another sphere of illustration. Within that representation of daily Christian life he took Mount Sinai as the occasion for introducing two other mountains from within Israel, Zion and Tabor, in order to construct a lively application of the Wittenberg understanding of the life of daily repentance. Sinai clearly stands for the law of God which holds sinners accountable for their sins and condemns them. As the mountain of the temple in Jerusalem, Zion symbolizes the gospel of the forgiveness of sins won by Christ through his death and resurrection. Tabor, according to medieval legend the mountain on which Jesus was transfigured, represents the liberation of the believer

59 *Margarita theologica*, 120. Cyriakus edited a meditation on baptism from his father's hand a decade later, *Ein Geistlich Badt der Seelen/ angezeigt im Leiblichen Bade/ Durch spru[e]che der Schrifft bewert* (Magdeburg: Michael Lotther, 1552).

60 Although many of Luther's students did not emphasize this sacrament as the Reformer himself did (see Tranvik, "The Other Sacrament"), Spangenberg certainly did.

61 Peters, *Kommentar zu Luthers Katechismen, Bd. 3*, 100-103.

from this world of sin and death. The rhythm of law and gospel was to govern the practice of the faith.

SPANGENBERG'S POLEMIC AGAINST MEDIEVAL PIOUS PRACTICES

Spangenberg concluded his treatise with a series of questions regarding what he viewed as abuses of medieval piety under the title "On the Knighthood of the Papists." In fact, these questions did not utilize the image of the knight at all. They provided readers with a straightforward critique of selected practices on the basis of Spangenberg's own examination of Bible passages used to defend them.

Both Evangelicals and Roman Catholics put this kind of popular polemic (the art of controversial criticism) to use in attempting to win the allegiance of the common people and to reinforce the convictions of those already won to their side. Since the earliest days of Christianity, theologians had attempted to clarify the truth of their own positions by contrasting that truth with the false positions they opposed.[62] In addition, polemical exchange played important roles in late medieval university life. The disputation, the academic equivalent of the knights' tournament, provided the setting for young scholars to "win their scholarly spurs" by defending theses formulated by themselves or their professors against their instructors and fellow students. Promotion from one academic level to the next degree took place on the basis of such disputations. Sharp critical intellectual exchange was a habit of mind for theologians as well as all other members of university faculties. When Luther's challenge to medieval teaching and practice reached the ears or eyes of his peers at universities across Germany and Europe, those who opposed him reacted with the tools of their trade, including pointed polemical critique. Indeed, those who realized the seriousness of Luther's appraisal of the faults of the medieval Church felt that he threatened the order of society and the salvation of their people. On the other hand, Luther felt that his call to reform should win the support of the leaders of the Church. When pope and bishops instead condemned him and began burning his followers at the stake for heresy, he reacted with a deep sense of betrayal that whetted his polemical rapier. Spangenberg reflected this attitude.

---

62 Gensichen, *We Condemn.*

In his little books Luther sought to lead readers and hearers away from certain fundamental beliefs that had shaped medieval piety. One of these fundamental presuppositions, as the Wittenberg reformers identified it, depicted the Christian as the object of mechanical sacramental action, a belief that too often led the faithful to think that their own faith in God played little role in their relationship to him. Sacraments were believed to bestow grace or power to accomplish both spiritual and temporal goals. They were said to work *ex opere operato*, that is, automatically through the performance of the ritual. Though not the original intent of this doctrine, which had aimed at preserving the validity of God's working in the sacraments apart from human manipulation, this view had led to magical practices, especially in connection with the Lord's Supper. Another medieval presupposition taught that a Christian's good works can win God's favor and forgiveness and offset the liability incurred by sinning. Much of medieval pious practice sought to win God's grace through the performance of ecclesiastical prescriptions for ritual religious actions and virtuous moral conduct.

In contrast to these assumptions, Luther taught that God works through his Word (indeed, in sacramental as well as oral and written forms) in conversation with his human creatures. God effects his will by placing judgment on sin through the Word of his law and by bestowing forgiveness of sins, life, and salvation through the Word of his gospel. Perhaps the most important insight of the Wittenberg Reformer was his observation that Scripture presumes that human creatures live in two different dimensions. They fulfill God's plan for them in relationship to himself through simple trust toward their Creator, and they fulfill his plan for them in relationship to other human creatures through love for their neighbors (Matt. 22:37-40). They are fully human, that is, in his terminology "righteous," in God's sight only because God loves them in Jesus Christ, has chosen them in Christ to be his own, and—through the gospel that delivers the benefits of Christ's death and resurrection to them—reconstitutes their identity as his children. Luther was convinced that trusting in Christ motivated the good works. The performance of these works of love constitutes human righteousness in relation to God's world.[63]

The practices that Spangenberg rejected included the veneration of relics and related customs that he regarded as magical and contrary to living in faith in the work of Christ. That critique lay at the root of his

63   Kolb, "Luther on the Two Kinds of Righteousness."

critique of the Mass as a sacrifice as well. His instruction on how to use Scripture shaped his examination of the Bible passages with which a series of practices were defended by theologians of the Roman Catholic Church: sprinkling with holy water, the daily regimen of prayer of the monks, Masses for the dead, purgatory, pilgrimages, brotherhoods, and other such practices. He also criticized Catholic opponents' claims for the authority of the hierarchy and of councils.

Luther and his Wittenberg colleagues had often combined their negative assessments of specific customs of the medieval Church with a doctrinal analysis of their bases. Spangenberg did not lead his readers into an evaluation of the ideas that underlay the practices he criticized. He did dismiss the biblical arguments behind some of them. In this way he was also cultivating his readers' ability to search the Scriptures. By identifying false interpretations as well as absorbing what God wanted to say to them, they, he was certain, would find eternal life. That, too, was part of the battle in behalf of God's truth that Spangenberg was describing.

The text of Johann Spangenberg's *Booklet of Comfort* gives twenty-first century readers a glimpse into the ways in which Martin Luther's followers and friends cultivated the piety of their contemporaries. Spangenberg sought to engage pastors and lay people in the midst of their daily lives with a program for pious living and confident dying that actualized the vision of Luther and his Wittenberg colleagues for the Christian Church. Students of the Reformation can gain from this booklet a deeper comprehension of how the early adherents of the Wittenberg Reformation shaped their teaching for consumption in daily life.

❧

Those who use this book as an exercise in early modern High German should note some peculiarities of the orthography. In the sixteenth century "u" and "v" were understood as essentially the same letter, "v" usually the form of the letter when used at the beginning of a word, "u" used often internally. Likewise, "i" and "j" are the internal and initial forms of the same letter in many cases although an "i" is used in this text at the beginning of some words, such as "ist," quite frequently. Punctuation in sixteenth-century German texts consisted of question marks, periods, and slashes (/). The slashes reflect the predominantly oral use of printed texts: they indicate where a pause should come for

effective conveying of the meaning of the text. The super-imposed "e" above the vowels "a," "o," and "u" is rendered in this volume with an "e" in brackets after the letter, following widespread modern editing practice, to reduplicate as closely as typographically possible what stands in the sixteenth-century text. This form is the equivalent of the modern umlauted letters, "ä," "ö," and "ü." Latin phrases have been left in Latin in the translation since they were in a foreign language also for sixteenth-century German readers. In the sixteenth century there was no standard German orthography. Words that appear outside the range of normal variation are followed by [!].

The work was printed in octavo format, that is, eight pages were printed on each side of one large leaf of paper. Page designations convert what is actually on the leaf to a standardized form.

The *New Revised Standard Version* of the Bible has been used when the original German text did not require an independent translation.

BIBLIOGRAPHY

Sixteenth-Century Printings

Full bibliographical entries for sixteenth century-publications are found in the footnotes, particularly those which list the published works of Johann Spangenberg. This is not a complete bibliography of his works. For such a bibliography, see *Verzeichnis der im deutschen Sprachbereich erschienenen Drucke des XVI. Jahrhunderts*. Ed. Bayerische Staatsbibliothek in München and Herzog August Bibliothek in Wolfenbüttel, 1. Abt., Bd. 19. Stuttgart: Hiersemann, 1992: 392-433 (#S7749-S8098).

Edited Sources

Die Bekenntnisschriften der evangelisch-lutherischen Kirche. Göttingen: Vandenhoeck & Ruprecht, 1930, 1991.

Bernhard von Clairvaux, Sämtliche Werke lateinisch/deutsch I. Ed. Gerhard B. Winkler. Innsbruck: Tyrolia, 1990.

The Book of Concord. Ed. Robert Kolb and Timothy J. Wengert. Minneapolis: Fortress, 2000.

Erasmus, Desiderius. *Collected Works of Erasmus, Spiritualia, Enchiridion, De Contemptu Mundi, De Vidua Christiana.* Vol. 66. Ed. John W. O'Malley. Toronto, Buffalo, London: University of Toronto Press, 1988: 1-23 (introduction), 24-127 (text).

————. *Erasmus. Handbook of the Militant Christian.* Trans. John P. Dolan. Notre Dame, IN: Fides, 1962.

Jonas, Justus. *Der Briefwechsel des Justus Jonas.* Ed. Gustav Kawerau, 1. Halle, 1884/ Hildesheim: Olms, 1964.

Luther, Martin. *D. Martin Luthers Werke.* Weimar: Böhlau, 1883-1993.

————. *Luther's Works.* Saint Louis and Philadelphia: Concordia and Fortress, 1958-1986.

Melanchthon, Philip. *Corpus Reformatorum. Opera quae supersunt omnia.* Ed. C. G. Bretschneider and H. E. Bindseil. Halle and Braunschweig: Schwetschke, 1834-1860.

Reu, Johann Michael, ed. *Quellen zur Geschichte des Katechismus-Unterrichts,* 2, *Mitteldeutsche Katechismen,* 2. Abt. Gütersloh, 1911, Hildesheim: Olms, 1976.

Wackernagel, Philipp, ed. *Das deutsche Kirchenlied von der ältesten Zeit bis zu Anfang des XVII. Jahrhunderts* 3. Leipzig: Teubner, 1870.

LITERATURE

Althaus, Paul, Sr. *Forschungen zur Evangelischen Gebetsliteratur.* Gütersloh: Bertelsmann, 1927.

Appel, Helmut. *Anfechtung und Trost im Spätmittelalter und bei Luther.* Leipzig: Heinsius, 1938.

Barth, Hans-Martin. *Der Teufel und Jesus Christus in der Theologie Martin Luthers.* Göttingen: Vandenhoeck & Ruprecht, 1967.

Bornkamm, Heinrich. *Luther and the Old Testament.* Trans. Eric W. and Ruth C. Gritsch. Philadelphia: Fortress, 1969.

Dingel, Irene. "'Recht glauben, Christlich leben, und seliglich sterben,' Leichenpredigt als evangelische Verkündigung im 16. Jahrhundert." In *Leichenpredigten als Quellen historischer Wissenschaft,* 4. Ed. Rudolf Lenz (Stuttgart: Steiner, 2004): 9-36.

Dost, Timothy P. *Renaissance Humanism in Support of the Gospel in Luther's Early Correspondence.* Aldershot: Ashgate, 2001.

Edwards, Mark U. Jr. *Printing, Propaganda, and Martin Luther.* Berkeley: University of California Press, 1994.

Elze, Martin. "Züge spätmittelalterlicher Frömmigkeit in Luthers Theologie." *Zeitschrift für Theologie und Kirche* 62 (1965): 381-402.

Falk, Franz. *Die deutschen Sterbebüchlein von der ältesten Zeit des Buchdruckes bis zum Jahre 1520.* Cologne: Bachem, 1890.

Fischer-Galati, Stephen A. *Ottoman Imperialism and German Protestantism 1521-1555.* Cambridge, MA: Harvard University Press, 1959.

Frei, Hans. *The Eclipse of Biblical Narrative, A Study in Eighteenth and Nineteenth Century Hermeneutics.* New Haven: Yale University Press, 1974.

Gensichen, Hans Werner. *We Condemn, How Luther and 16th Century Lutheranism Condemned False Doctrine.* Trans. Herbert J. A. Bouman. Saint Louis: Concordia, 1967.

Hamm, Bernd. *Lazarus Spengler (1479-1534), Der Nürnberger Ratsschreiber im Spannungsfeld von Humanismus und Reformation, Politik und Glaube.* Tübingen: Mohr Siebeck, 2004.

Jones, Ken Sundet. "*Promissio* and Death: Luther and God's Word for the End of Life." Ph.D. dissertation, Luther Seminary, Saint Paul, 2003.

Junghans, Helmar. *Der junge Luther und die Humanisten.* Göttingen: Vandenhoeck & Ruprecht, 1985.

Kawerau, Gustaf. "Spangenberg, Johann." in *Real-Encyklopädie für protestantische Theologie und Kirche.* Ed. Albert Hauck, 18 (Leipzig: Hinrichs, 1906: 563-567).

Koch, Ernst. "Spangenberg, Johann," in *Religion in Geschichte und Gegenwart*[4] 7 (Tübingen: Siebeck Mohr, 2004): 1536.

Kolb, Robert. "Johann Spangenbergs 'Christlicher Ritter' als Beispiel der frühlutherischen Erbauungsliteratur." *Lutherische Theologie und Kirche* 28 (2004): 57-80.

———. "Luther on the Two Kinds of Righteousness. Reflections on His Two-Dimensional Definition of Humanity at the Heart of His Theology." *Lutheran Quarterly* 13 (1999): 449-466.

———. "Parents Should Explain the Sermon, Nikolaus von Amsdorf on the Role of the Christian Parent." *The Lutheran Quarterly*, o.s. 25 (1973): 231-240.

———. "'Saint John Hus' and 'Jerome Savonarola, Confessor of God,' The Lutheran 'Canonization' of Late Medieval Martyrs." *Concordia Journal* 17 (1991): 404-418.

———. "'What Benefit Does the Soul Receive from a Handful of Water?' Luther's Preaching on Baptism, 1528-1539." *Concordia Journal* 25 (1999): 346-363.

Leaver, Robin A. "Luther as Musician." *Lutheran Quarterly* 18 (2004): 125-181.

Leppin, Volker. "'Omnem vitam fidelium penitentiam esse voluit'—Zur Aufnahme mystischer Traditionen in Luthers erster Ablassthese." *Archiv für Reformationsgeschichte* 93 (2003): 7-25.

Leuckfeld, Johann Georg. *Verbesserte Historische Nachricht von dem Leben und Schrifften M. Johann Spangenbergs*, 1720, a facsimile in *Historia Leuckfeldi oder ausführliche Beschreibung von Leben und Werk des Johann Georg Leuckfeld*. Ed. Carsten Berndt. Auleben: Regionale-Verlag, 2003.

Merzbacher, Friedrich. "Militia Christi." *Lexikon der christlichen Ikonographie* 3 (Rome: Herder, 1971/1994): 267-268.

———. "Ritter." *Lexikon der christlichen Ikonographie* 3 (Rome: Herder, 1971/1994): 554-556.

Miller, Gregory J. "Luther on the Turks and Islam." *Lutheran Quarterly* 14 (2000): 79-97.

Moeller, Bernd. *Deutschland im Zeitalter der Reformation*, 2. ed. Göttingen: Vandenhoeck & Ruprecht, 1981.

———. "Frömmigkeit in Deutschland um 1500." In idem, *Die Reformation und das Mittelalter, Kirchenhistorische Aufsätze*. Ed. Johannes Schilling. Göttingen: Vandenhoeck & Ruprecht, 1991: 73-85.

Mohr, Rudolf. "Ars moriendi II," *Theologische Realencyklopädie*. Ed. Gerhard Krause and Gerhard Müller 4 (Berlin/New York: de Gruyter, 1979): 149-154.

———. "Erbauungsliteratur III." *Theologische Realencyklopädie*. Ed. Gerhard Krause and Gerhard Müller 10 (Berlin/New York: de Gruyter, 1982): 51-80.

Panofsky, Erwin. *Albrecht Dürer, Volume One*. Princeton: Princeton University Press, 1943.

Peters, Albrecht. *Kommentar zu Luthers Katechismen, Bd. 3, Das Vaterunser*. Ed. Gottfried Seebaß. Göttingen: Vandenhoeck & Ruprecht, 1992.

Post, Regnerus R. *The Modern Devotion. Confrontation with Reformation and Humanism*. Leiden: Brill, 1968.

Reinis, Austra. "Reforming the Art of Dying: The *Ars Moriendi* in the German Reformation (1519-1528)." Ph. D. dissertation, Princeton University, 2003.

Rudolf, Rainer. *Ars Moriendi. Von der Kunst des heilsamen Lebens und Sterbens*. Cologne/Graz: Böhlau, 1957.

Schulz, Freder. "Gebetsbücher III." *Theologische Realencyklopädie*. Ed. Gerhard Krause and Gerhard Müller 12. (Berlin/New York: de Gruyter, 1984): 109-119.

Spitz, Lewis W. *The Religious Renaissance of the German Humanists*. Cambridge MA: Harvard University Press, 1963.

Stolt, Birgit. *Wortkampf. Frühneuhochdeutsche Beispiele zur rhetorischen Praxis*. Frankfurt/M: Athenäum, 1974.

Tranvik, Mark David. "The Other Sacrament: The Doctrine of Baptism in the Late Lutheran Reformation." Th. D. Dissertation, Luther Northwestern Theological Seminary, Saint Paul USA, 1992.

Tschackert, Paul. "Spangenberg, Johann." In *Allgemeine Deutsche Biographie* 35 (Leipzig: Duncker & Humblot, 1893): 43-46.

[AIR] EIN NEW TROST
BU[E]CHLIN FUR DIE KRANCKEN VND /
VOM CHRISTLICHEN RITTER:

DURCH M. JOHANN SPANGENBERG.

1548

A BOOKLET OF COMFORT FOR THE SICK, AND
ON THE CHRISTIAN KNIGHT

BY JOHANN SPANGENBERG

1548

DEM EHRWIRDIGEN HERRN
PETRO SEDRIANO / ABT ZU DER PFORTEN / MEINEM BE-
SONDERN LIEBEN HERREN VND FREUNDE.

Gnad vnd Fried / durch Jhesum Christum vnsern HErrn.
Erwirdiger herr / besonder lieber Freund vnd Patron / Nach
dem Gott der Almechtige in diesen ferlichen zeiten / das arme
heufflin seiner Christen / nicht allein mit der Veterlichen ruten / mit
Kriege vnd Theurung / Pestilentz / vnd andern vngehorten kranckheiten
/ sondern auch mit der Eisern ruten / mit dem grimmigen wu[e]ten des
Tu[e]rcken / heimsucht / Wil von no[e]ten sein / das wir vns widder
solche grewliche Bu[e]lge vnd Sturmwinde / allenthalben mit Gottes
wort ru[e]sten vnd tro[e]sten / vnd wo es Gottes wille ist / auch wil-
liglich vnd gerne [A2v] sterben / vnd wiewol ein Christ weis / aus den
schrifften des lieben S. Pauli / Er lebe oder sterbe / das er des HErrn sey
/ So hats doch mu[e]he vnd erbeit / angst vnd not / wenn das sterben
furhanden ist / Denn da ringt vnd windet sich der alt Adam / vnd stirbt
vngern / das die zeit freilich tro[e]stens vnd vermanens wol not ist /
auff das der sterbende Mensch / sich willig inn Gottes willen ergebe. Es
haben aber diese zeit daher / viel tapffer gelerte Menner vom sterben
geschrieben / welcher Bu[e]cher / dieweil sie ein jderman nicht beko-
men mag / hab ich etliche vbersehen / vnd diese kurtze vnterrichtung
(selig zu sterben) draus genomen / Dieselbige / aus bitte etlicher guter
freunde / inn Frage stu[e]cke verfasset / vnd Ewer Erwirden dedicirt

To the Honorable Lord Peter Sedrianus, abbot at
the Gates, my special, dear lord and friend.[1]

Grace and peace through Jesus Christ, our Lord.
Most honorable lord, particularly dear friend and patron,
since God the Almighty is visiting his poor little flock of Christians not only with the fatherly rod of war and hard times, plague and other unheard-of diseases, but also with the furious rage of the Turk,[2] it is necessary that we outfit ourselves for every occasion with God's Word against the terrifying billows and storm winds and find comfort in his Word, and if God wills, die willingly and gladly. Although every Christian knows from the writings of beloved Saint Paul that whether he lives or dies, he is the Lord's [Rom. 14:8], nonetheless, the Christian experiences pain and grief, fear, and distress when death draws near. For when the Old Adam[3] wriggles and writhes, resisting death, that is the time when comfort and exhortation are necessary so that the dying person surrenders willingly to God's will. For this reason in these times many well-respected learned men have written on the subject of dying. Because not everyone has access to these books, I have looked through several of them and drawn from them this brief instruction on dying in a blessed manner. At the request of several good friends, I have compiled it in question and answer form. I am dedicating it to Your Worthiness

---

1 In line with the custom of the time Spangenberg probably expected financial support from this abbot in return for the dedication of this work to him.

2 Perhaps the most significant threat to Christian Europe and particularly the German Empire at Spangenberg's time was the Ottoman Turkish empire, which had conquered Constantinople in 1453 and had held large parts of the Balkan Peninsula south and east of Hungary since the fourteenth century. In 1526 Turkish forces defeated the Hungarian army at the Battle of Mohacs, and in 1529 they laid siege to Vienna. See Gregory J. Miller, "Luther on the Turks and Islam," and Stephen A. Fischer-Galati, *Ottoman Imperialism and German Protestantism*.

3 A frequently used term among Lutherans to designate the sinful nature that fights against the reborn nature in the baptized Christian, based upon Romans 5:12-21.

vnd zugeschrieben / auff das die jungen Christen / beide / knaben vnd meidlin / durch [A3r] Ewer Erwirden / ein kurtze form haben / sich vntereinander zu fragen / vnd also diese kunst / des sterbens / welche furwar nicht die geringste kunst ist / jnn der jugent wol einbilden vnd fassen mo[e]gen / Bitte / Ewer Erwirde wolle diesen meinen armen dienst / nicht verschmehen / sondern diese kleine Gaben / zum seligen newen Jare / freundlich annemen.

Christus vnser lieber Hirte vnd Heiland / jnn welches hand / Leben vnd Tod steht / wolle Ewer Erwirden / jnn reiner Lere / vnd Gottseligem leben / gnediglich erhalten. Datum Northausen / 1542. am tage Nicolai des heiligen Bisschoffs.

    Ewer Erwirden
        vntertheniger.
        M. Johannes Spangenberg

so that young Christians, both boys and girls,[4] will have a short form for asking each other about the art of dying through [the generosity of] Your Worthiness. It is indeed not the least significant skill which young people may impress upon their minds and digest for themselves. I entreat Your Worthiness not to disdain my meager service but kindly accept this small gift for a blessed new year.

Christ, our dear shepherd and savior, in whose hand lie life and death, graciously preserve Your Worthiness in pure teaching and a God-pleasing life.

Nordhausen, on the day of the holy bishop Nicholas,[5] 1542.

Your Worthiness's servant,
Master Johannes Spangenberg

---

4 In line with his goal and purpose for most of his publications, Spangenberg prepared this treatise for those whom he instructed in school as part of his duties as a parish pastor. In sixteenth-century society children often encountered death and the necessity of bringing comfort to the dying.

5 The festival of Saint Nicholas is December 6.

[A3v] Wie sich ein Mensch bereiten sol zu einem seligen sterben / Eine Christliche vnterrichtung / jnn Fragstu[e]cke verfasset / durch M. Joannem Spangenberg.

Wie mancherley ist das sterben?
Zweierley. Eins ist ein zeitlichs / das ander ein ewigs / sterben.

Was ist das zeitlich sterben?
Nichts anders / denn wenn leib vnd seel von einander scheiden.

Was ist das ewige sterben?
Nichts anders / denn wenn die seele von Gott mus scheiden. Vnd das heist der ewige Tod.

Wie mancherley ist der Tod?
Zweierley. Ein zeitlicher / vnd ein ewiger Tod.

Was ist der ewige Tod?
Der ewige Tod / ist ein zertrennung / Gottes vnd der Seele / ein [A4r] ewig schrecken des menschlichen Gewissens / fur dem zorn Gottes / vnd ein entliche verzweiuelung an Gottes gnaden.

Was ist der zeitliche Tod?
Der zeitliche Tod / ist der letzte abschied / von dieser Welt / vnd ein entlicher beschlus / aller menschlichen hendele / wie der Poet sagt / Mors vltima linea rerum est.

Woher ist der Tod in die welt komen?
Aus des Teuffels hass vnd neid / eben die zeit / da Adam vnd Eua / Gottes gebot vbertraten / vnd von den verboten fru[e]chten des Paradises / assen. Denn der bissen hat Adam vnd all seine kinder / jnn angst

How people should prepare for a blessed death.
Christian instruction,
composed in questions and answers.
By Master Johannes Spangenberg

How many kinds of dying are there?
There are two kinds of dying. One is temporal death, the other eternal death.

What does it mean to die temporally?
Nothing else than when the body and soul separate from each other.

What is eternal dying?
Nothing else than when the soul must separate from God. That is called eternal dying.

How many kinds of death are there?
Two: temporal death and eternal death.

What is eternal death?
Eternal death is a separation between God and the soul, eternal terror for the human conscience in the face of God's wrath, and ultimate despair of God's grace.

What is temporal death?
Temporal death is the last farewell from this world and a final conclusion of all human activities, as the poet says, "*Mors ultima linea rerum est.*"[6]

Where did death come from when it came into the world?
From the devil's hate and envy at the time when Adam and Eve transgressed God's commandment and ate of the forbidden fruits of paradise [Gen. 3:1-7]. For that bite brought Adam and all his children

---

6 "Death is the end to which all things are moving," a quotation from the Latin poet Horace.

vnd not / mu[e]he vnd erbeit / jamer vnd elend bracht / ja den Tod
auffgeerbt. Denn also sagt das Buch der Weisheit am andern Capitel /
Gott hat den Menschen geschaffen zum ewigen Leben / Vnd [A4v] hat
jn gemacht zum bilde / das er gleich sein sol / wie er ist / Aber durch
des Teuffels hass vnd neid / ist der Tod in die Welt komen.

Jst denn niemand sicher fur dem Tode?
Kein lebendiger Mensch / Wir Mu[e]ssen alle ein mal sterben Hebre.
9. vnd wenn wir schon so viel Jar lebten / als Mathusalem / Nemlich
/ neunhundert vnd neun vnd sechtzig jar / so mu[e]ssen wir doch zu
letzt sterben. Moises erzelet viel jar der Ertzueter / Nemlich / Adam
hab gelebt neunhundert vnd dreissig jar. Seth / neunhundert vnd
zwo[e]lff jar. Enos / neunhundert vnd fu[e]nff jar. Noha / neunhundert
vnd funfftzig jar etc. Aber allezeit beschleust er / Et mortuus est / Er
ist gestorben.

Fu[e]rcht denn der Tod kein gewalt noch kunst?
Der Tod achtet weder gewalt noch kunst / noch reichtumb. Du
[A5r] seiest Gewaltig / Reich / Klug oder weise / so mustu doch
sterben. Der Tod fragt nicht nach der Tyrannen wu[e]ten / Auch nicht
nach der Reichen gu[e]ter. Fragt nicht nach der Juristen schweren /
Auch nicht nach der Sophisten disputirn. Der Tod achtet nicht der
Papisten drawen / Auch nicht den pracht der scho[e]nen Frawen. Er
acht auch nicht das trauren der armen / vnd jn summa / er lesst sich
keins Menschen erbarmen. Er felt so bald in des Keisers Pallast / Als
jnn eines armen Hirten haus. Ja wo sind hin alle Bepste / Patriarchen
vnd Primaten. Alle Cardinel Bisschoff vnd Prelaten. Pro[e]bste / De-

into fear, misery, trouble, toil and affliction; yes, it bequeathed them death. For the book of Wisdom says in chapter two [:23-24],[7] God created human beings for eternal life and made them in his image that they might be like him, as he is. But through the devil's hate and envy death came into the world.

Is then no one secure in the face of death?

Not a single living human being. We must all die sometime, Hebrews 9 [:27]. And even if we have already lived so many years as Methuselah, 969 [Gen. 5:25-27], we must finally die at last. Moses lists many years for the patriarchs: Adam lived 930 years [Gen. 5:3-5], Seth 912 years [Gen. 5:6-8], Enos 905 years [Gen. 5:9-11], Noah 950 [Gen. 9:28-29], etc. But each time he concluded, *Et mortuus est*, "he died."

Does death then fear no power or ability?

Death does not pay attention to power nor to a person's ability nor to riches. You may be powerful, rich, intelligent, or wise, but you still have to die. Death does not take the rage of tyrants nor the possessions of the rich into account. It does not take the oaths of the jurists into account, and it does not take the disputations of the sophists into account. Death does not pay any attention to the threats of the papist nor to the finery of beautiful women. It does not pay attention to the sorrow of the poor. In summary, it has mercy on no human being. It falls as quickly upon the emperor's palace as upon the house of a poor shepherd. Where have all the popes gone?[8] all the patriarchs and primates,

---

7 Modern readers may be surprised to find citations from the Apocryphal book of Wisdom in Spangenberg's work. Luther had indeed followed the Hebrew canon rather than that of the Septuagint, the Greek translation of the Old Testament, and excluded the Apocrypha from his canon. He had included these books, however, in his translation of the Bible, grouped after the Old Testament books that appear in the Hebrew Bible, and had explained that although he did not regard them as part of the biblical canon, he found them useful and edifying writings. His followers continued to cite some of the Apocrypha, particularly Wisdom and Jesus Sirach, throughout the sixteenth and into the seventeenth century.

8 Spangenberg here draws on a popular literary and artistic motif of medieval Europe, expressed, for instance, in the "Dance of Death" series of paintings of several artists. This motif shows that death visits all people, of every walk of life.

chant / Thumbpfaffen. Vicarien / Chorschu[e]ler / vnd der gleichen maulaffen. Ebte / Priors vnd Gardianten / Lector Lolhart vnd ander bachanten. Doctores / Magistri / vnd Licentiaten / Baccalaurien / [A5v] Studenten vnd Locaten? Wo sind hin alle Keiser / Ko[e]nige / Fu[e]rsten / Landsherrn. Graffen / Ritter vnd Banerherrn. Alle Edele / Bu[e]rger vnd Ackerleute. Frawen / Jungfrawen vnd alle Breute. Alle Handwercksmeister vnd knechte. Ja das gantze menschlich geschlechte? Wo ist Paris vnd Helena? Tarquinius vnd Lucretia? Wo ist Plato vnd Porphirius? Wo ist Tullius vnd Vergilius? Wo ist Tales vnd Empedocles?

all cardinals, bishops and prelates, all deans and cathedral priests, vicars and choir boys and the fools of that sort, abbots, priors, and guardians, lector Lolhard[9] and other vagabonds, doctors, masters, and licentiates, bachelors, students and classmates? Where have all emperors gone, all the kings, princes, nobility, counts, knights, and standard bearers? All nobles, citizens, and farmers, mistresses, virgins, and brides? All of the master artisans and their servants? Yes, the entire human race? Where are Paris[10] and Helen,[11] Tarquinius[12] and Lucretia?[13] Where are Plato[14] and Porphry?[15] Where are Tullius[16] and Virgil?[17] Where are Thales[18]

---

9 Walther (or Nikolaus) Lolhard (or Lollard) was a legendary heretic, said to have been burned in Cologne in 1322 for a variety of false teachings.

10 Paris was a figure in Greek mythology, a Trojan prince who launched the Trojan War by kidnapping Helen after judging Aphrodite the most beautiful of the goddesses and thus winning the right from her to the world's most beautiful woman.

11 Helen was a figure in Greek mythology, daughter of Zeus and Leda, wife of the Greek king of Sparta Menelaos, who led the Greeks to war against Troy after his wife was kidnapped by Paris.

12 Tarquinius here refers to Tarquinius Sextus, son of the legendary seventh king of Rome Tarquinius Superbus (534-510 B.C.), who lost the royal throne as a result of the rape of Lucretia by his son.

13 Lucretia was a legendary figure in early Roman history, whose rape by Tarquinius Sextus led to the fall of the first Roman dynasty.

14 Plato (427-347 B.C.), the influential Greek philosopher, student of Socrates, teacher of Aristotle.

15 Porphry (ca. 234-305), a student of Plotinus, was a prominent neoplatonic philosopher and commentator on the works of Plato and Aristotle.

16 Marcus Tullius Cicero (106-43 B.C.) was a Roman statesman, orator, and influential author, whose thought influenced the thinking of many of Spangenberg's contemporaries.

17 Vergil (Publius Vergilius Maro) (70-19 B.C.) was a poet and leading interpreter of the legendary past of Rome.

18 Thales of Milet (ca. 640 or 624- ca. 545 B.C.) was a pre-Socratic Greek philosopher, whose works were read throughout the Middle Ages.

vnd der grosse meister Aristoteles? Alexander der Ko[e]nig / gros vnd
theur. Hector / der Troianer schutz vnd maur? Wo ist Julius der Keiser
gut. Priamus / Achilles das edel blut? Wo ist der starcke Samson? vnd
der weise Salomon. Der schnelle Azahel / vnd der scho[e]ne Absolon?
Sie sind alle dahin / Durch todes krafft vnd pein. Adam ist gestorben
/ dem mu[e]ssen all seine kin- [A6r] der volgen. Auch das kind eines
tages / oder einer stunde / Jst gleich im selbigen Bunde. Summa / sie
mu[e]ssen alle in todes pein / So viel jr in der welt geboren sein.

Das ist furwar ein arme elende sache?
Freilich elend. Darumb sage auch jener Philosophus / Das es gut
were / der mensch wu[e]rde nicht geboren / oder stu[e]rbe so balde
nach der geburt Der mensch ist freilich am besten dran / der bald ans
ende seins lebens ko[e]mpt / der ist von vielen sorgen / mu[e]he vnd
arbeit / erlo[e]st.

and Empedocles?[19] Where is the great master Aristotle?[20] Alexander[21] the great and beloved king? Hector,[22] the protection and the defense of the Trojans? Where is Julius, the good emperor,[23] Priam,[24] Achilles[25] of noble blood? Where is the mighty Samson [Judg. 13:24-16:31]? And the wise Solomon [see especially 1 Kings 3], the fleet-footed Asahel [2 Sam. 2:18], and the handsome Absalom [2 Sam. 13-19]? They have all passed away through the power and the pain of death. Adam died, and all his children must follow him. The child who is one day old or even an hour old is in the same bag. In summary, as many as are born into this world must experience the pain of death.

That is really a miserable, wretched state of affairs, is it not? It is indeed miserable. Therefore, the philosopher says that it would be good if human beings would never be born or would die as soon as they were born [Eccl. 4:1-3]. The human being who reaches the end of life quickly is indeed in the best situation. Such a person is delivered from many cares, from much exertion and toil.

---

19   Empedocles (483/482-430/420 B.C.) was a pre-Socratic Greek philosopher, whose works were read throughout the Middle Ages.

20   Aristotle (384-322 B.C.) was, with Plato, the Greek philosopher who exercised the deepest and most widespread influence on medieval philosophy and theology.

21   Alexander the Great (356-323 B.C.), son of King Philip of Macedonia, student of Aristotle, established the largest empire to that date by conquering most of the eastern Mediterranean world and the Persian Empire.

22   Hector was a figure in Greek mythology, son of King Priam and Queen Andromache, a Trojan hero who fell in a duel with Achilles.

23   Julius Caesar (100-44 B.C.) was a Roman general and statesman, who expanded Roman holdings in a series of wars, became dictator of Rome, and was assassinated. He did not claim the title "emperor," but his nephew, Augustus, did, introducing the imperial form of government to Rome.

24   Priam was a figure in Greek mythology, king of Troy, father of one hundred children, including Hector and Paris.

25   Achilles was a figure in Greek mythology, who killed Hector but was killed by Paris when he learned that Achilles was vulnerable only in his heal.

Was ist des menschen leben?

Nichts anders / denn ein teglicher kampff vnd Ritterschafft hie auff erden / Job 7. Das menschliche leben / ist einem Schiff gleich. Du gehest odder stehest / sitzest odder ligest im Schiffe / so gehests fur sich hin / zum vfer zu. Also faren [A6v] wir auch jnn diesem leben / vnter den menschlichen hendeln dahin / bis jnn Tod.

Hat denn der Tod keine gewisse zeit?

Nein. Das sterben ist gewis / aber die stunde ist vngewis. Niemand sol sich beku[e]mmern / wo / odder wenn er sterben sol / Wir sind dem Tode ein sterben schu[e]ldig / Wo der vns anspricht / es sey im holtze odder felde / im hause / oder hoffe / draussen odder daheim / da mu[e]ssen wir bezalen / Ein jder sehe nur darauff / das er mit der bezalung geschickt sey.

So ho[e]re ich wol / wir mu[e]ssen schlechts sterben?

Da wird nicht anders aus / wir haben alle des Leinkauffs getruncken / Gott hat die seel jnn den leib gossen / mit dem gedinge / Wenn er sie fodert / das sie bereit sey / Dieweil aber die foderung vngewis ist / [A7r] vnd wissen nicht / welchen tag / odder welche stunde / vns Gott foddern wil / so sollen wir / vmb eines vngewissen tages / vnd vmb einer vngewissen stunde willen / alle tage vnd stunde / jnn acht haben / auff das er vns nicht vnbereitet finde.

Wie sol ich mich denn zum seligen sterben bereiten?

Hieuon / sind viel Bu[e]cher geschrieben / Aber ich wil dir einen kurtzen bericht thun.

Dis sol die erste bereitung sein.

Ein Christ (wes standes er ist) sol hie am leben / seinen Beruff / Stand vnd Ampt / also verbringen / in einem rechten glauben / in

What is human life?

Nothing else than a daily battle and contest here on earth, Job 7 [:1-10]. Human life is like a ship. Whether you are moving or whether you are standing still, whether you are sitting or lying down in a ship, it keeps on moving along toward the shore. And so, as the human affairs slog on, we make our way in this life toward death.

Is the time of death fixed?

No. It is certain that we must die, but the hour of our death is not certain. No one should be concerned about where or when he will die. We have a debt to pay to death. Wherever death initiates the conversation with us, whether in the woods or a field, whether in a house, farmyard, outside or at home, there we must pay. Each person should just see to it that he is prepared to pay.

So, do I hear correctly: we must simply die?

There is no other way out. We have all drunk a toast to this arrangement.[26] God has poured the soul into the body with the condition that, when he demands it, it should be ready [to die]. And because it is uncertain [when] this demand [will come], and we do not know on which day or at which hour our God will make the demand of us. Just because of this uncertainty of the day and hour, we should be alert every day and hour, so death does not find us unprepared.[27]

How can I prepare for a blessed death?

On that subject many books have been written, but I will give you a brief review.

This is the first preparation.

A Christian, in whatever walk of life,[28] should carry out his calling, walk of life, and responsibility in true faith, in brotherly love, and in

26 A "Leikauff" or "Leinkauff" was a toast which completed a business agreement.

27 When Spangenberg writes of the uncertainty of the hour of death, he is speaking from the human perspective. He believed that God had fixed the times of people's lives.

28 "Stand" in German, usually translated into English "estate," was the basic category of medieval social theory, which understood human life as unfolding in three "walks of life," the estate or situation of family and economic life

bru[e]derlicher liebe / in to[e]dtung des alten Adams / das er mit einem fro[e]lichen hertzen / vnd gutem gewissen fur Gott / im sterben bestehen ko[e]nde / Denn / wer recht vnd wol lebt / der stirbt auch wol / Gott gebe / er sterbe draussen / odder daheim / im [A7v] holtze / odder felde. Der Mensch kan nicht vbel sterben / der allezeit wol gelebt hat. Einem guten leben volget kein bo[e]ser tod.

So werden die reichen vnd gewaltigen wol sterben / denn sie leben stets wol?

Wol leben / heisset hie / Christlich leben / Nicht / wie die welt wol lebt. Wol sterben / heisset gerne sterben. Gerne sterben / bringt der Glaube. Wol sterben / bringen die fru[e]chte des glaubens.

Wie so?

Wer in Gott gleubt / vnd hertzlich vertrawet / vnd darneben ein Christlich leben vnd wandel fu[e]rt / der stirbet nicht vngern / Denn er weis / wohin er faren sol / Nemlich / dem lieben Vater jnn den Schos / Wie Christus sagt Johan. 17. Vater / ich wil / wo ich bin / das auch meine Diener da sein. Stirbt auch nicht vbel / Denn Christus wird zu [A8r] jm / vnd zu allen auserwelten sagen / Kompt her / jr gesegneten meines Vaters / ererbt das Reich / das euch bereitet ist / von anbegin der welt / Jch bin hungerig gewesen / vnd jr habt mich gespeiset etc.

Jch fu[e]rchte mich aber fur dem tode / vmb etlicher vrsach willen?

Du hast vielleichte gehort den Spruch / den die welt pfleget zu reimen.

> Drey ding ligen mir hart an
> Jch mus sterben vnd weis nicht wann /
> Jch fare / vnd weis nicht wohin
> Wie kan ich jmer fro[e]lich sein.

the mortification of the Old Adam, so that he can undergo death with a joyous heart and a good conscience before God. For the person who lives properly and well, dies well, whether God determines that he die away from home or at home, in the woods or in the field. The person who has always lived a good life cannot experience an evil death. A bad death does not follow a good life.

So the rich and powerful experience a good death since they have always had a good life?
To live a good life means in this case a Christian life, not a good life in the sense of this world. To die well means to die willingly. Faith produces [the ability] to die willingly. The fruits of faith produce [the ability to have] a good death.

How is that?
Whoever believes in God and trusts with all his heart, and then lives and conducts life in a Christian way, does not die unwillingly. For he knows where he is going, namely, to the lap of his dear Father, as Christ says in John 17 [:24], "Father, I desire that those also, whom you have given me, may be with me where I am." Such a person does not experience an evil death, since Christ will say to him and all the elect, "Come to me, you blessed of my Father, inherit the kingdom that has been prepared for you, from the beginning of the world, for I was hungry, and you fed me," etc. [Matt. 25:34-40].

[What if] I am afraid of death for other reasons?
Perhaps you have heard the proverb, which the world likes to sing,

> Three things weigh heavy on my heart:
> I must die and do not know when.
> I depart and do not know to where.
> How can I be ever happy?

(in Latin *oeconomia*), the civil sphere or secular government (*politia*), and the church (*ecclesia*). Many medieval thinkers taught that each person is placed in one of these situations, according to the person's chief occupation. Luther taught that each person has responsibilities in each. Spangenberg's usage here seems closer to the traditional medieval interpretation.

Dis ist ein Heidnischer spruch / der sol fern von einem Christen sein / Denn wir wissen wol (wie vor gesagt ist) wo wir hin sollen / Nemlich / dem lieben Vater in den schos. So spricht S. Paulus / Wir leben odder sterben / so sind wir des HERRN.

[A8v] Jch fu[e]rchte aber den Tod / vmb meiner vnuersorgten kinder willen.

Versorge deine kinder / weil du noch am leben bist / Kere allen vleis an / das du sie jnn Gottes furcht / im glauben / vnd in der liebe / auffziehest / vnd las sie lernen den Catechismum / Sind sie tu[e]chtig zu der Lere / so halt sie zur Schule / las sie gute ku[e]nste vnd sitten lernen / das sie der Christenheit dienen mo[e]gen / mit leren / predigen etc. Wo nicht / so las sie ehrliche handwercke lernen / das sie nicht mu[e]ssig gehen / vnd auff eines andern beutel / prassen vnd zeren / vnd dru[e]ber zu buben / dieben / vnd Reubern werden / sondern jderman dienen / beide / im Obern vnd vntern Stande. Sihe / da stirbstu mit freuden / vnd ererbest deinen kindern einen gnedigen barmhertzigen Gott / vnd ein vnsterblich ewig Erbteil / Denn aller welt gu[e]ter / Reichthumb / vnd gewalt [B1r] sind vergenglich / aber Ku[e]nste vnd Tugent / bleiben ewig.

Welche ist die ander Bereitung / seliglich zu sterben?

Das du der Welt vnd aller Creaturen liebe / auch dein selbs / vmb Gottes willen absagest / Also / das du dich nicht weiter beku[e]mmerst / mit den zeitlichen dingen dieser welt sondern dich fro[e]lich alles erwegest / vnd dich bereitest auff den Weg / vnd zu der Pforten einzugehen / jnn das ewige Leben / zu deinem lieben Schepffer vnd Vater / Denn wer hindurch wil / der mus aller zeitlichen sorge / ledig sein / vnd sich willig vnd gern verzeihen / der lust vnd liebe aller Creaturen / vnd alles was auff Erden ist.

Was sol vns zu solcher absagung erinnern?

Der Eyd / den wir Gott geschworen haben / jnn der Tauffe / da wir entsaget haben / dem Teu- [B1v] ffel / der Welt / vnd allen lu[e]sten der Creaturen. Jtem / der spruch Jobs am ersten Capitel / Jch bin nacket von meiner mutter leib komen / nacket werde ich widder dahin faren. Jtem / der spruch S. Paulus 1. Timo. 6. Wir haben nichts jnn die Welt bracht / darumb offenbar ist / wir werden auch nichts hinaus bringen / Wenn wir aber futter vnd decke haben / so lasset vns benu[e]gen.

This is a pagan proverb. Such thoughts should be the farthest thing from a Christian's mind. For we know (as has already been said) where we are going, namely to the lap of our dear Father. So Paul said, "Whether we live or die, we are the Lord's" [Rom. 14:8].

I fear death because my children will not be taken care of.

Take care of your children while you are still alive. Be very sure that you raise them in the fear of God, in faith, and in love, and have them learn the catechism. If they are able to learn well, keep them in school. Have them learn good skills and proper behavior, so that they may serve their fellow Christians with teaching, preaching, etc. If they cannot do that, let them learn an honest trade, [and see to it] that they are not lazy, and do not carouse and waste money out of someone else's purse. Beyond that, [see to it] that they do not become criminals, thieves, and robbers. Rather [see to it] that they serve everyone, both in the higher and lower walks of life. Then, you will die with joy and bequeath your children a gracious, merciful God and an immortal, eternal legacy. For the riches of the goods of the whole world and its power pass away, but skills and virtues remain forever.

What is the second way to prepare to die in a blessed fashion?

You [must] renounce your love of the world and everything that has been created, and even of yourself, for the sake of God. That is, you do not concern yourself further with the temporal things of this world but think everything through with no illusions, and prepare yourself to travel on the way to the gates [that lead] into eternal life, to your dear Creator and Father. For whoever wants to go this way must be free of all temporal worry and be willing [to die], gladly relinquishing the desire for and love of everything created and everything on earth.

What should call this renunciation to mind?

The oath which we have sworn to God in baptism, where we have repudiated the devil, the world, and all desires for things God has made. Thus, the words of Job in his first chapter [:21] "Naked I came from my mother's womb, and naked I will return there," and Paul's words, 1 Timothy 6 [:7], "We brought nothing into the world; therefore, it is clear, we can take nothing out of it; but if we have food and clothing, we will

Diese / vnd der gleichen Spru[e]che / sollen wir / die gantze zeit vnsers lebens / wol bedencken / Vnd sonderlich / wenn wir sollen von hinnen scheiden.

Es ist aber ja die Pforte zu enge / vnd der Weg zu schmal?
Ob die Pforte wol enge / vnd der Weg schmal ist / so ist er doch nicht lang / Vnd gehet hie zu / wie Christus von dem schwangern weibe sagt Johan. 16. Ein Weib / wenn sie gebirt / so hat sie traurig- [B2r] keit / denn jre stunde ist komen / Wenn sie aber das kind geboren hat / dencket sie nicht mehr an die angst / vmb der freude willen / das der Mensch zur Welt geboren ist. Also mu[e]ssen wir auch dencken / das nach diesem eusserlichen leben / werde ein gro[e]sser raum sein / im ewigen Leben / Vnd hie auff diesem Wege gilt es / gewonnen odder verloren / Wer hie gewinnet / der hat ewig gewonnen / Wer hie verleuret / der hat ewig verloren.

Worinne stehet dis Absagen der Welt?
Jnn zweien dingen. Zum ersten / das du deine gu[e]ter / schulde vnd handel / also verordenest / das nach deinem abschied / kein zanck vnter deinen kindern vnd freunden erwachsse. Zum andern / das du die jenige / so du beleidiget hast / vmb vergebung bittest / Vnd widerumb denen / die dich beleidiget haben / [B2v] vmb Gottes willen verzeihest. Wenn solchs geschehen ist / als denn kere dich mit gantzem hertzen zu Gott / vnd sihe nicht widder zu ru[e]cke / gen Zodoma vnd Gomorra / mit Lots weibe / Auch nicht jnn Egypten / mit den kindern Jsrael / sondern las faren / alles was nicht bleiben wil / sol odder kan / vnd mache dich fein leicht / auff den Weg zum rechten Vaterlande / Da werden wir keinen vnlust / sondern hundertfeltige erstattung haben / aller der dinge / die wir von hertzen faren lassen / wie vns denn Christus gantz tro[e]stlich verheisset / Matth. 19. Wer da verlesset Heuser / odder Bru[e]der / oder Schwestern / oder Vater / oder Mutter / oder Weib / oder Kind / oder Ecker / vmb meines Namens willen / der wirds hundertfeltig nemen / vnd das ewige Leben ererben.

be content." We should think on these and other similar passages our entire life, and especially when we are about to depart from here.

But isn't the gate too small and the path too narrow?

Even if the gate is too small and the path too narrow [Matt. 7:14], it certainly is not long, and it gets there quickly, as Christ said of the pregnant woman in John 16 [:21], "When a woman is in labor, she has pain, because her hour has come. But when her child is born, she no longer remembers the anguish because of the joy of having brought a human being into the world." Therefore, we must remember that after this earthly[29] life, there will be a greater dwelling place in eternal life. Here, on this way, you win or you lose, and who wins here has won eternally, and whoever loses here has lost eternally.

In what does the renunciation of the world consist?

In two things. First, that you put your goods, your debts, and your business affairs in order, so that after your departure no argument arises among your children and friends.[30] Second, that you ask for forgiveness from those to whom you have done wrong, and on the other hand that you forgive those who have done wrong to you because it is God's will. When this has taken place, then turn toward God with your whole heart, and do not look back to Sodom and Gomorrah with Lot's wife [Gen. 13:26], nor to Egypt with the children of Israel [Ex. 17:3]. Let all that pass that cannot, should not, nor will not remain, and without a second thought make your way to our real fatherland. There we will not be in misery, but instead [we will receive] a hundredfold compensation for all the things that we have let depart from our hearts, as Christ promised in his very comforting way, Matthew 19 [:29], "Everyone who has left houses or brothers or sisters or father or mother or children or fields for my name's sake will receive a hundredfold and will inherit eternal life."

---

29   "Äusserlich" literally means outward but refers to the regular course of daily life on this earth, before death, in contrast to the "inward" or spiritual life in relationship with God, both before and after death.

30   Many medieval authors urged the dying not to think on earthly matters at all and therefore discouraged them from making the arrangements involved in a last will and testament. Spangenberg follows Luther in advising this as an exercise of Christian responsibility to the neighbor.

Welche aber dermassen nicht sterben / Wie wirds den gehen?

[B3r] Die da vermeinen Christen zu sein / vnd hangen noch an diesen Creaturen / vnd scheiden mit vnwillen / ja offt mit halb verzweiueltem hertzen / die verlieren alhie die zeitlichen gu[e]ter / vnd dort / die ewigen / Hie das zeitliche leben / vnd finden dort den ewigen Tod. Darumb sollen die Christen / jr lebenlang / allen Creaturn / lernen absterben / welche sie von der Liebe jres Schepffers / abziehen mo[e]gen.

Das ist schwer / sich aller Creaturen / lust vnd liebe / zu verzeihen / vnd blos an Gott hangen?

Wie schwer es ist / so mus doch der mensch sich entlich drein begeben / das er willig faren lasse / alles zeitliches / vnd willig sterbe.

Das ist aber menschlicher natur vnmu[e]glich?

War ists / Wenn aber der mensch jnn einem festen glauben / die Artickel / Vergebung der sunde / Auffer- [B3v] stehung der Todten / vnd des ewigen Lebens / ergreifft / vnd dieselbigen stets bedenckt / so ists jm nicht vnmu[e]glich / Denn da weis er / das Christus eben darumb fur vns gestorben / vnd aufferstanden ist / auff das er vns frey vnd ledig machete / von dem ewigen Tod / vnd vns mit jm entlich fu[e]re / in das ewige Leben / Derhalben auch vnser leiblicher Tod / in der Schrifft / nicht tod / sondern ein schlaff / genennet wird / vnd ein Friedefart / vnd Ruge / von aller mu[e]he vnd arbeit / an leib vnd seele.

Welche ist die dritte Bereitung / zu sterben?

Du solt dir etliche Trostspru[e]che / aus der Schrifft vnd Euangelio / wider alle anfechtunge / wol einbilden / vnd zum vorrad versamlen / vnd stets bey dir im hertzen tragen / Gleich wie ein Schu[e]tz / seine pfeile im Ko[e]cher tregt / vnd [B4r] zur notturfft behelt / vnd braucht.

Was sol vns darzu erinnern?

Zum ersten / der spruch Christi Matth. 25. vnd Marci 13. Sehet zu / wachet vnd betet / denn jr wisset nicht / wenn des menschen Son komen wird / am abend / oder zu mitternacht / oder vmb das Hanenge-

How will it be for those who do not die in this way?

There are those who think that they are Christians but still cling to what is created and depart unwillingly, indeed often with hearts that are halfway in despair. They lose the temporal blessings of this earth and the eternal blessings of heaven. They lose temporal life here and find eternal death there. Therefore, throughout their entire lives Christians should be learning to die to what is created, to those things that might draw them away from the love of their Creator.

It is difficult to lay aside desire and love for everything created and cling only to God, is it not?

No matter how difficult it is, a person must finally give in, so that he willingly lets go of everything temporal and dies willingly.

But is that not impossible for human nature?

That is true. But when a person grasps the articles of faith regarding the forgiveness of sin, resurrection of the dead, and everlasting life[31] with a firm faith and continually keeps them in mind, then it is not impossible. For such a person knows that Christ has died and has arisen for us in order to liberate us and make us free from eternal death and to lead us into eternal life with him in the end. Therefore, in Scripture our bodily death is not called death but a sleep, a peaceful journey, and a rest from all tribulation and toil in body and soul.

What is the third preparation for dying?

You should impress some comforting passages from Scripture and the gospel on your memory, passages to use against all temptations. Collect them as provisions [for the journey] and always carry them with you in your heart, just as a soldier carries his arrows in the quiver and has them ready to use whenever he needs them.

What should remind us of that?

First, the words of Christ in Matthew 25 [:1-46, cf. 24:42-44] and Mark 13 [:35-36], "Keep awake, watch and pray, for you do not know when the Son of Man will come, in the evening, or at midnight, or when

---

31 "Articles of faith" refers to individual teachings or doctrines of the church. Here Spangenberg lists three such teachings explicitly rehearsed in the third article of the Apostles' Creed.

schrey / odder des morgens / das er nicht schnell kome / vnd finde euch schlaffend. Zum andern / der spruch S. Peters 1. Petri 5. Lieben bru[e]der / seid nu[e]chtern vnd wachet / denn ewer Widersacher der Teuffel gehet vmbher / wie ein bru[e]llender Lewe / vnd suchet / welchen er verschlinge / dem widderstehet feste im glauben. Zum dritten / der spruch S. Pauli Ephe. 6. Meine lieben bru[e]der / seid starck in dem HErrn / Zihet an den harnisch Gottes / das ir bestehen ku[e]nd / gegen dem listigen anlauff des Teuffels / Ergreifft [B4v] den Harnisch Gottes / auff das jr widderstehen ku[e]nd / an dem bo[e]sen tage / So stehet nu / vmbgu[e]rtet ewere lenden mit warheit / vnd angezogen mit dem krebs der Gerechtigkeit / vnd gestieffelt an fu[e]ssen / mit dem Euangelio des Friedes / Fur allen dingen aber / ergreifft den Schilt des Glaubens / mit welchem jr ausleschen kund / alle feurige pfeile des Bo[e]sewichts / vnd nempt den Helm des Heils / vnd das Schwerd des Geistes / welches ist das Wort Gottes / vnd betet stets / jnn allem anligen / vnd wachet darzu mit allem anhalten vnd flehen.

Fur was anfechtunge sol ich Trostspru[e]che samlen?
Fur die anfechtung allerley Kranckheit / Verfolgung / Marter vnd pein / Fur die anfechtung des Teuffels / Tods / Su[e]nde vnd der Helle.

Gib Trostspru[e]che fur die kranckheit?
[B5r] Der 46. Psalm sagt / Gott ist vnser zuuersicht vnd stercke / eine hu[e]lffe inn den grossen no[e]ten / die vns troffen haben. Vnd Salomon inn Spru[e]chen am 3. Capitel sagt / Mein kind / verwirff die zucht des HERRn nicht / vnd sey nicht vngedu[e]ltig / vber seiner straffe / Denn welchen der HERR strafft / den hat er lieb / vnd hat wolgefallen an jm / wie ein Vater am Son. Und S. Paulus Roma. 8. So wir mit leiden / werden wir auch mit herrschen / Jch halts aber dafur / das dieser Zeit Leiden / der Herrligkeit nicht werd sey / die an vns sol offenbar werden. Desgleichen soltu hie dem krancken / mit allem vleis / das Vater vnser fursprechen / vnd die bitte (Dein wil geschehe / als im Himel / also auch auff Erden) wol einbilden.

Gib Trostspru[e]che / fur die verfolgunge vnd marter.
[B5v] Der 116. Psal. sagt / Der tod seiner Heiligen / ist werd ge-halten fur dem HErrn. Vnd im buch der Weisheit am 5. Capitel / Als denn wird der Gerechte stehen mit grosser freidigkeit widder die / so

the cock crows, or at the dawn, or else he may find you asleep when he comes suddenly."[32]

Second, the words of Saint Peter, 1 Peter 5 [:8-9], "Dear brothers, like a roaring lion your adversary the devil prowls around, looking for someone to devour. Resist him, steadfast in the faith." Third, the passage from Saint Paul, Ephesians 6 [:10-11, 13-17], "My dear brothers, be strong in the Lord. Put on the whole armor of God so that you may be able to stand against the wiles of the devil.... Take up the whole armor of God so that you may be able to withstand on that evil day .... Stand, therefore, and fasten the belt of truth around your waist, and put on the breastplate of righteousness. As shoes for your feet put on the gospel of peace. With all of these take the shield of faith, with which you will be able to quench all the flaming arrows of the Evil One. Take the helmet of salvation, and the sword of the Spirit, which is the Word of God. Pray at all times in every situation, and keep alert with steadfastness and prayer."

For what kind of temptations should I collect these passages of comfort?

For the temptations of all kinds: of illness, persecution, suffering, and pain, of the temptations of the devil, death, sin, and hell.

[Can you] give some passages of comfort for illness?

Psalm 46 [:1] says, "God is our refuge and strength, a very present help in trouble." Solomon in Proverbs, chapter three [:11-12], says, "My child, do not despise the Lord's discipline or be weary of his reproof, for the Lord reproves the one he loves, as a father the son in whom he delights." And Saint Paul in Romans 8 [:17-18], "If we suffer with him, we will also reign with him. I consider that the sufferings of this present time are not worth comparing with the glory that will be revealed to us." At the same time the Lord's Prayer should be carefully said aloud to the sick person, and the petition "Thy will be done on earth as in heaven" properly explained.

Give some passages of comfort for persecution and affliction.

Psalm 116 [:15] says, "Precious in the sight of the Lord is the death of his holy people." And in the Book of Wisdom 5 [:1, 4-5], "Then the righteous will stand with great boldness against those who have

32 Spangenberg here weaves together words from Matthew and Mark.

in geeng stet haben / vnd sein Erbe verworffen haben etc. Wir Narren hielten sein Leben fur vnsinnig / vnd sein Ende fur ein schande / Sihe / wie ist er nu gezelet vnter die kinder Gottes / vnd sein Erbe ist vnter den Heiligen etc. Vnd Christus sagt Matthei 5. Selig sind / die vmb der Gerechtigkeit willen verfolget werden / denn das Himelreich ist jr etc. Vnd Matt. 10. Fu[e]rcht euch nicht fur denen / die den leib to[e]dten / vnd die seele nicht mo[e]gen to[e]dten / Fu[e]rcht euch aber viel mehr fur dem / der leib vnd seel verderben mag / in die Helle / Keufft man nicht zween sperlinge vmb einen pfenning? noch felt derselbigen keiner auff die Erden / on [B6r] ewern Vater / Nu aber sind auch ewer hare / auff dem heubt alle gezelet / Darumb furcht euch nicht / jr seid besser denn viel sperlinge.

Gib Trostspru[e]che / fur die anfechtung des Teuffels?
Christus sagt Matth. 16. Auff diesen Fels (vernemet auff Christum) wil ich Bawen meine Gemein / Vnd die Pforten der Hellen sollen sie nicht vberweltigen. Vnd Luce am 10. Capitel / Jch hab euch macht geben / zu tretten auff schlangen vnd scorpion / vnd vber allen gewalt des Feindes / vnd nichts wird euch beschedigen. Vnd 1. Johan. 4 Kindlin / jr seid von Gott / vnd habt jene vberwunden / Denn der in vns ist / der ist gro[e]sser / denn der in der Welt ist. Vnd S. Paulus spricht 1. Corin. 10. Gott ist trew / der euch nicht lesset versuchen / vber ewer vermu[e]gen / sondern macht neben der versuchung / ein auskomen / das jrs ku[e]nd vertragen.

[B6v] Gib Trostspru[e]che / fur das schrecken vnd furcht des Todes?
Der Prediger Salomon sagt am 7. Capitel / Der tag des todes ist besser / denn der tag der geburt / Denn der tag der geburt bringt mit sich allerley jamer / an leib vnd seele Der tag aber des sterbens (so wir im rechten Christlichen Glauben sterben) endet dis alles. Vnd Christus spricht Johan. 5. Warlich / warlich / ich sage euch / Es ko[e]mpt die stunde / vnd ist jtzt / das die todten werden die stimme des Sons Gottes ho[e]ren / Vnd die sie ho[e]ren werden / die werden leben etc. Vnd S. Paulus 1. Corinth. 15. aus dem Propheten Ozea sagt / Der Tod ist verschlungen jnn dem sieg / Tod wo ist dein stachel? Helle wo ist dein sieg? Aber der stachel des Todes / ist die Su[e]nde / Die krafft aber der sunde / ist das Gesetz. Gott aber sey danck / der vns den sieg ge- [B7r] geben hat / durch vnsern HERRN Jhesum Christum.

made them afraid and have repudiated his inheritance." etc. "We fools regarded his life as madness and his end as a scandal. Behold, now he is counted among the children of God, and his inheritance is among the saints." And Christ says in Matthew 5 [:10], "Blessed are those who are persecuted for righteousness' sake, for theirs is the kingdom of heaven," etc. And Matthew 10 [:28-31], "Do not fear those who kill the body but cannot kill the soul; rather fear him who can destroy both soul and body in hell. Are not two sparrows sold for a penny? Yet not one of them will fall to the ground apart from your Father. And even the hairs of your head are all counted. So do not be afraid; you are of more value than many sparrows."

[Can you] give some passages for assaults of the devil?

Christ says, Matthew 16 [:18], "On this rock (that refers to Christ) I will build my community, and the gates of hell shall not overcome it." And Luke 10 [:19], "I have given you the power to tread on snakes and scorpions, and over all the power of the enemy, and nothing will hurt you." And 1 John 4 [:4], "Little children, you are from God and have conquered them, for the one who is in us is greater than the one who is in the world." And Saint Paul says, 1 Corinthians 10 [:13], "God is faithful, and he will not let you be tested beyond your strength, but with the testing he will also provide the way out, so that you may be able to endure it."

[Can you] give passages of comfort for terror and fear in the face of death?

The preacher Solomon says, [Ecclesiastes] 7 [:1], "The day of death is better than the day of birth." For the day of birth brings along with it every kind of misery for body and soul. The day of death, on the other hand, ends all of this (if we die in true Christian faith). And Christ says, John 5 [:25], "Very truly I tell you, the hour is coming, and is now here, when the dead will hear the voice of the Son of God, and those who hear will live." And Saint Paul cites from the Prophet Hosea, 1 Corinthians 15 [:55-57, cf. Hos. 13:14], "Death has been swallowed up in victory. Where, O death, is your stinger? Hell, where is your victory? The stinger of death is sin, and the power of sin is the law. But thanks be to God, who gives us the victory through our Lord Jesus Christ." And in 1 Thessalonians 4 [:13-14], "We do not want you

Vnd zu den Thessalonichern am 4. jnn der ersten / Wir wollen euch / lieben Bru[e]der nicht verhalten / von denen die da schlaffen / auff das jr nicht traurig seid / wie die andern / die keine hoffnung haben / Denn so wir gleuben / das JHesus gestorben / vnd aufferstanden ist / so wird Gott auch / die da entschlaffen sind durch Jhesum / mit jm fu[e]ren etc. Vnd zun Philippern am 1. Cap. Christus ist mein leben / vnd sterben ist mein gewin / Jch habe lust abzuscheiden / vnd bey Christo zu sein.

Gib Trostspru[e]che / wider die anfechtung der Hellen?
Der Prophet Ozea sagt am 13. Capitel / Jch wil sie aus der Helle erlo[e]sen / vnd vom Tod erretten / Tod ich wil dein gifft sein / Helle / ich wil dir eine plage sein. Vnd Christus sagt Johan. 3. Wer an den [B7v] Son gleubt / der wird nicht gericht / Wer aber nicht gleubt / der ist schon gericht / Wer an den Son gleubt / der hat das ewige Leben / Wer an den Son nicht gleubt / der wird das Leben nicht sehen / sondern der zorn Gottes bleibt vber jm. Vnd Johan 5. Warlich / warlich / ich sage euch / wer mein Wort ho[e]ret / vnd gleubt Dem / der mich gesand hat / der hat das ewige Leben / vnd ko[e]mpt nicht jnns Gerichte / sondern er ist vom Tode zum Leben hindurch gedrungen. Vnd am 11. Capitel / Jch bin die Aufferstehung vnd das Leben / Wer an mich gleubt / der wird leben / ob er gleich stu[e]rbe / vnd wer da lebt vnd gleubt an mich / der wird leben / ob er gleich stu[e]rbe / Vnd wer da lebt vnd gleubt an mich / der wird nicht sterben ewiglich. Vnd S. Paulus Rom. 8. So ist nu nichts verdamlich an denen / die in Christo Jhesu sein / die nicht nach dem fleisch wandeln / sondern nach dem Geist / [B8r] So nu der Geist / des / der Jhesum vom Tode erwecket hat / jnn euch wonet / So wird auch derselbige / der Christum von den todten aufferwecket hat / ewere sterbliche Leibe lebendig machen / vmb des willen / das sein Geist in euch wonet. Vnd im Buch der Weisheit / stehet geschrieben am 3. Capitel / Der Gerechten Seelen / sind in der hand Gottes / vnd sie wird nicht beru[e]ren die pein des Todes. Vnd Christus Johan. 9. spricht / Warlich / warlich sage ich euch / So jemand wird mein Wort halten / der wird den Tod nicht sehen ewiglich.

Welche ist die vierde Bereitung / seliglich zu sterben?
Du solt dich erinnern deiner Tauff / vnd wie du dich damit Gott verbunden hast / Nemlich / das du wilt entsagen / dem Teuffel vnd all seinem anhange / Gleuben in Gott [B8v] Vater / Son / vnd den Heiligen

to be uninformed, dear brothers, about those who have fallen asleep, so that you may not grieve, as others do who have no hope. For as we believe that Jesus died and rose again. Even so through Jesus, God will bring with him those who have fallen asleep." And Philippians 1 [:21-23 summarized], "Christ is my life, and death is my gain. I desire to depart and be with Christ."

[Can you] give passages of comfort against the assaults of hell?
The prophet Hosea says in chapter 13 [:14], "I shall redeem them from hell and rescue them from death. Death, I will be your poison. Hell, I will be your destruction." And Christ says, John 3 [:18], "Whoever believes on the Son is not condemned. Whoever does not believe is already condemned. Whoever believes on the Son has eternal life. Whoever does not believe on the Son will not see life, but the wrath of God remains upon him." And John 5 [:24], "Anyone who hears my word and believes him who sent me has eternal life and does not come under judgment but has passed from death to life." And John 11 [:25-26], "I am the resurrection and the life. Whoever believes on me will live, even if he dies, and whoever lives and believes will not die eternally." And Saint Paul in Romans 8 [:1, 9-11], "There is therefore no condemnation for those who are in Christ Jesus, who do not live according to the flesh but according to the Spirit. If therefore the Spirit of the one who raised Jesus from the dead dwells in you, he who raised Christ from the dead will give life to your mortal bodies through his Spirit who dwells in you." And in the Book of Wisdom is written in the third chapter [:1] "The souls of the righteous are in the hand of God, and the pains of death will not touch them." And Christ says in John 9 [8:51], "Very truly, I tell you, whoever keeps my word will never see death."

What is the fourth way to prepare to die a blessed death?
You should recall your baptism and how you bound yourself through it to God. To be precise, you want to repudiate the devil and all his gang, and to believe in God, Father, Son, and Holy Spirit, and to demonstrate

Geist / Vnd solchen Glauben auch beweisen / mit den fru[e]chten des
Glaubens / gegen den Menschen / Den alten Adam / das Su[e]ndliche
fleisch to[e]dten / vnd die bo[e]sen lu[e]ste vnd begirde dempffen /
vnd von tage zu tage / eine newe Creatur Gottes werden.

Wie sol ich mich aber mit meiner Tauff tro[e]sten?

Also soltu bey dir dencken vnd sagen / Sihe / darzu bistu getaufft /
vnd in dis leben gestelt / das du solt anfechtung vnd widderwertigkeit
leiden / nach dem Exempel deines Heilmachers Christi / Vnd dein
Creutz auff dich nemen / vnd jm volgen. Du hast in der Tauff Brieff
vnd sigil empfangen / das dein anfechtung / Creutze / Leiden vnd Tod
/ nicht dein / sondern Christus anfechtung / Creutze / Leiden vnd Tod
sind / Also / wie Christus [C1r] dasselbige alles hat vberwunden / vnd
ist entlich wider von den todten aufferstanden / vnd lebt ewiglich / das
du dermassen auch solt Teuffel / Tod / Su[e]nde vnd Helle / vnd alles
vbel / im Namen Gottes vberwinden / vnd am Ju[e]ngsten tage wider
erweckt werden / von den todten / vnd mit Christo ewig leben. Das
hat dir der Priester vber der Tauff zugesagt / im Namen des Vaters /
des Sons / vnd des Heiligen Geistes. Dieser zusage / wird er dir nicht
entpfallen / Denn er ist ein warhafftiger Gott.

Welche ist die fu[e]nffte Bereitung / seliglich zu sterben?

Gedenck an die krafft des hochwirdigen Sacraments des Leibs vnd
bluts Christi / das du empfangen hast / vnd wirff alle dein anligen /
beschwerung / angst vnd tru[e]b [C1v] sal / in den Schos der Christlichen Kirchen / vnd schrey zu Gott also.

O Almechtiger / Ewiger / barmhertziger Gott / Jch bin leider ein
grosser Su[e]nder / bin gefallen jnn dis vnd das Laster / jnn Hoffart /
geitz / vnzucht / hass / neid etc. Mich dru[e]ckt dis vnd jens vnglu[e]ck
/ Hab diese vnd die beschwerung etc. Nu kan ich von mir selbs keinen
Trost vberkomen / Hie lige ich jnn deiner gewalt / vnd kan mir selber
nicht helffen / Darumb mein gu[e]tiger Gott / Jch ero[e]ffne dir mein
hertze / vnd klage dir meine Su[e]nde / mein angst vnd anligen / Auff
deine Go[e]ttlichen Zusage / hab ich empfangen das hochwirdige Sacrament / als ein gewis zeichen / das du mir wilt gnedig vnd barmhertzig
sein / vnd all meine su[e]nde vergeben. Jch gleub auch / das du mit all
deinen auserwelten / bey mir stehest / Sol ich [C2r] sterben / so werde
ich nicht allein im tode sein / Sol ich leiden / so werden sie alle mit mir

this faith as well, with the fruits of faith toward other people, to mortify the Old Adam, the sinful flesh, and to subdue the evil desires and longings, and from day to day become a new creature of God.

But how am I to find comfort in my baptism?

You should think to yourself and say to yourself, "Look, you are baptized, and in this life you are likely to suffer temptation and hostility, following the example of your savior Christ." You are to take your cross upon you and follow him [Matt. 16:24]. In your baptism you have received a promise signed and sealed that your temptation, cross, suffering, and death do not belong to you, but they are Christ's temptation, cross, suffering, and death. That means, as Christ has conquered all of them, and in the end he rose from the dead and lives eternally, so in the very same way you shall conquer the devil, death, sin and hell and every evil in the name of God, and awake again on the Last Day from the dead and live with Christ eternally. The priest promised you that in your baptism in the name of the Father and of the Son and of the Holy Spirit. He will not go back on this promise to you, for he is a faithful God.

What is the fifth way to prepare for a blessed death?

Think about the power of the holy sacrament of the body and blood of Christ that you have received, and cast all other concerns, burdens, fears, and tribulations into the lap of the Christian church, and cry to God in this way:

O almighty, eternal, merciful God, I regret that I am a bad sinner. I have fallen into this and that vice, into arrogance, greed, fornication, hatred, envy, and so forth. This and that misfortune are weighing me down. I have this or that burden and so forth. I cannot find any comfort on my own. I lie here in your power and am unable to help myself. Therefore, my gracious God, I open my heart to you, and pour out my sins, my fears, and my concerns before you. Upon your divine assurance I have received the holy sacrament as a certain sign that you want to be gracious and merciful and forgive all my sins. I also believe that you stand by me, as you stand by all your chosen people. Should I die, I will not be alone in death. Should I suffer, they will all suffer with me.

leiden / Des hab ich ein gewis zeichen empfangen / den waren Leib
vnd das theure Blut deines lieben Sons Jhesu Christi / vnter dem brod
vnd wein / Das zeichen wird mir nicht feilen / Jch las mirs auch nicht
nemen / vnd ob die gantze Welt widder mich stu[e]nde / Du mein
Gott / bist mir gewis genug / jnn dieser zusage / Jch sey wirdig odder
vnwirdig / da ligt nichts an / dennoch bin ich ein glied der Christenheit / auff den Felsen Christum / durch den Glauben gebawet / Es ist
noch besser / ich sey vnwirdig / denn das Gott nicht solte warhafftig
sein / Meiner su[e]nde wird wol radt / wenn ich allein seinem Worte
gleube / Dein lieber Son / vnd mein fromer Heiland / hat ja gesagt /
Kompt zu mir / die jr mu[e]heselig vnd beladen seid / Jch [C2v] wil
euch erquicken / vnd alle die zu mir komen (spricht er) die wil ich
nicht von mir stossen. Er spricht auch / Er sey vmb der Su[e]nder willen komen / Vnd wo[e]lle das zerstossen Rohr nicht zubrechen / vnd
das gliemende Tocht nicht follend ausleschen / Des tro[e]ste ich mich
/ darauff verlasse ich mich. Das sind Worte des warhafftigen Gottes /
die werden mir nicht feilen.

Wie / wenn mich die su[e]nde gleich wol anficht?
So gedenck an das vnschu[e]ldige Lamb Gottes / an JHesum Christum / der der welt su[e]nd getragen hat / Der fur vns worden ist
zur Gerechtigkeit / zur Heiligung / vnd zur Erlo[e]sung / Auff den
schu[e]tte alle deine su[e]nde. Denn durch seine gnad vnd gu[e]tigkeit
/ mu[e]ssen alle su[e]nde verleschen / wie ein fu[e]ncklin fewers im
grossen Meer verleschet.

[C3r] Jst denn Christus derhalben in die Welt komen?
Freilich darumb / auff das er aller Welt su[e]nde austilge. Wenn nu
die su[e]nde ausgetilget ist / so ist der Tod mit allen seinen krefften
vberwunden / Vnd hindert nicht / ob er noch vmbher schleicht /
wu[e]tet vnd tobet. Denn / wie ein Biene / die den stachel verloren hat
/ wol scharret vnd zornig ist / so kan sie doch nicht stechen. Also auch
/ Ob der Teuffel / Tod / Su[e]nd / vnd Helle / wol greulich drawen
/ vnd schrecken / so vermo[e]gen sie doch nichts / Die gifft ist jnen
genomen. So hat ein jeder Christ auch den trost / das er weis / das
Vater / Son / vnd Heiliger Geist (in welcher Namen er getaufft ist)
bey jm sein / jnn all seinem anligen / vnd fur jn streiten vnd kempffen
/ wider alle seine Feinde / sichtliche vnd vnsichtliche.

For this I have received a certain sign, the true body and the precious blood of your dear Son Jesus Christ, under the bread and wine. This sign will not let me down. I will not let it be taken from me. Even if the entire world stood against me, you, my God, are sufficient for me, with your promise. It does not depend on whether I am worthy or unworthy. Whatever the case, I am a member of the Christian church, built on Christ, the rock, through faith. It is better that I am unworthy than that God is not faithful. There will indeed be assistance against my sin if I just believe his Word. Your dear Son and my faithful savior has said, "Come to me, all you who are weary and carrying heavy burdens," [Matt. 11:28] and I will revive you. "I will not cast away those who come to me" [John 6:37]. "He will not break a bruised reed or quench a smoldering wick" [Matt. 12:20; Isa. 42:3]. In this I find comfort. I rely on these words. They are the words of God, who is faithful, and they will not let me down.

How is this possible when sin attacks me directly?

Think about the innocent lamb of God, on Jesus Christ, who has borne the sins of the world [John 1:29]. He has become our righteousness, our sanctification, our redemption [1 Cor. 1:30]. Pour out all your sins upon him. Through his grace and mercy all sins are extinguished by necessity as a spark of fire is extinguished in the immensity of the sea.

Did Christ come into the world for that purpose?

Indeed, precisely for that purpose, to obliterate the sins of the whole world. If sin has been obliterated, then death has been overcome with all its powers. It can do no more harm, even if it is still on the prowl, raging and raving. It is just like a bee that has lost its stinger; it may buzz and be enraged, but it still cannot sting.

For this reason, even if the devil, death, sin, and hell threaten and terrify [the Christian] in a horrible way, they cannot do anything! The poison has been taken out of them. So every Christian has the comfort of knowing that the Father, the Son, and the Holy Spirit (in whose name he has been baptized) is with him, in all that concerns him. They fight and wage the battle in his behalf against all his enemies, visible and invisible.

[C3v] Wenn mich aber der Tod noch wil erschrecken?

Warumb wiltu den Tod fu[e]rchten? Thut er doch dir die thu[e]r auff zum Ewigen Leben. Las die Vngleubigen vnd Gottlosen / den Tod fu[e]rchten / die durch den zeitlichen Tod gehen zum ewigen Tod. Las die fur dem Tod / Teuffel vnd Helle erschrecken / die Christum nicht zum Helffer vnd Heiland haben. Sprich du mit S. Paul / Jch weis wem ich gegleubt habe / hinfurt ist mir beigelegt / die Kron der Gerechtigkeit / welche mir der HERRE an jenem tage / der gerechte Richter geben wird / Nicht mir aber allein / sondern allen / die seine Erscheinung lieb haben.

Wie / wenn mich aber noch immerzu der Teuffel wil anfechten?

Las dichs nicht anfechten / stehe vnd bleib nur feste im Glauben / denn deine seligkeit ist gebawet auff [C4r] den harten felsen Christum / Dem mu[e]ssen alle Hellischen pforten weichen / Vnd sprich zum Teuffel also / Sihe Teuffel / Du fichst mich an / vnd thust mir viel zu leide / stehest mir nach Leib vnd Seele / Wolan / Mein Gott ist auch dein Gott / Jch bin Gottes Creatur / so wol als du / Wils nu mein Gott haben / das du mich solt anfechten / martern vnd plagen / so wil ichs vmb meines Gottes willen gerne dulden / Es verbiete dir aber mein Gott / das du mir auch an einem herlin leide thust on seinen willen / geschweige an meiner Seelen / Ja ich wil meinen fromen Gott bitten / das er mich / seine arme Creatur / fur deiner gewalt behu[e]te / vnd meine arme Seele nicht jnn deinen Rachen komen lasse / Hie lige ich in Gottes gewalt / vnd bin willig vnd bereit / zu leben vnd zu sterben / nach seinem Go[e]ttlichen wolgefallen / Jch kan mir selber [C4v] nicht helffen / habs auch nicht verdient / das er mir helffen sol / Aber doch gleub ich vnd hoffe / er werde mir helffen / vnd Mich aus gnaden selig machen / vmb seines lieben Sons / meines HERRn vnd Seligmachers Jhesu Christi willen / welcher fur mich vnd der gantzen Welt su[e]nde gestorben ist / vnd dafur gnug gethan hat / Vnd solches mir geschenckt / so ich an jn gleube / Ja nicht allein Mir / sondern allen Gleubigen / das ewige leben erworben. Des tro[e]ste ich mich / darauff verlasse ich mich / das ist mein einige hoffnung / Darauff bin ich getaufft / darauff hab ich das hochwirdige Sacrament des Leibs vnd Bluts Christi empfangen / Darauff wil ich auch friedlich vnd willig sterben / mit beistand seiner Go[e]ttlichen gnad vnd hu[e]lffe / Vnd wil hiemit meinen Geist befehlen vnd befohlen haben / in die hende mei- [C5r] nes himlischen Vaters / mit hertzlicher zuuersicht / Er werde Mich in keiner not verlassen /

But what if death still wants to terrify me?

Why do you want to fear death? It opens the door to eternal life for you. Let the unbelievers and the godless fear death, those who go through temporal death to eternal death. Let those who do not have Christ as their helper and savior be terrified in the face of death, devil, and hell. Say with Saint Paul, "I know the one in whom I have put my trust [2 Tim. 1:12]. From now on there is reserved for me the crown of righteousness, which the Lord, the righteous judge, will give me on that day, and not only to me but also to all who have longed for his appearing" [2 Tim. 4:8].

How is that possible if the devil keeps wanting to attack me?

Don't let him attack you. Stand firm in your faith and remain firm in your faith, for your salvation is built on the solid rock, Christ. The gates of hell must give way to him. Say to the devil, "Look, devil, you are attacking me and doing a lot to harm me. You are at my body and my soul. Just see here! My God is also your God. I am a creature of God, just as you are. If my God wills to have it so that you attack me, torture me, and torment me, I will gladly bear it for the sake of my God. But my God forbids you to do harm to a tiny hair of mine apart from his will, to say nothing of doing harm to my soul [Job 1:12, 2:6]. Yes, I will pray to my righteous God that he protect his poor creature in the face of your power and not let my poor soul into your jaws. I lie in God's power and am willing and prepared to live and to die according to his divine pleasure. I cannot help myself. I have not deserved it that he should help me. But I believe and hope that he will help me and save me by his grace for the sake of his dear Son, my Lord and Savior, Jesus Christ, who has died for me and for the sins of the whole world and has made satisfaction for them. He gives me this when I believe on him. Indeed, he has won eternal life not for me alone, but for all believers. I take comfort in that. I rely on that. That is my only hope. To that end I was baptized. To that end I have received the holy sacrament of Christ's body and blood. To that end I will also peacefully and willingly die, with the aid of his divine grace and help. I will commit my spirit to him and commend myself into the hands of my heavenly Father, with complete

noch ewiglich verdammen / Darumb schrey ich mit ho[e]chster begirde
zu Jhm / gleich wie Christus (mir zu tro[e]stlichen Exempel) am Creutz
thet / O Gott himlischer Vater / kom mir zu hu[e]lffe in der letzten
not. Jn deine hende befehl ich meinen Geist / Amen.

Gib mir eine kurtze Form / wie ich den sterbenden Menschen vermanen sol / zur gedult / vnd das er sich inn Gottes willen ergebe?

Sage erstlich also / Lieber Mensch / Gedenck / das du in diese Welt
komen bist / nicht das du drin bleiben solt / denn das were im elend
geblieben / Sondern das du (wenn Gott wil / dieses elenden lebens
mu[e]he vnd arbeit solt ablegen / durch ein zeitlich sterben) dich nicht
wei-[C5v] ter mit dieser Welt gu[e]tern / die vergenglich sind / Sondern
mit den hohen Himlischen dingen / ja mit dem ho[e]chsten gute / das
Gott selbs ist / beku[e]mmern / welchs nicht volkomen geschehen mag
/ es sterbe denn der alt Adam / Welch sterben dir vnd allen Menschen
gemein ist / Denn / wie wir alle mit Adam gesu[e]ndiget haben / Also
mu[e]ssen wir auch alle der su[e]nden straff / den tod leiden vnd tragen
/ vnd jhe gro[e]sser die kranckheit ist / jhe neher Gott ist mit seiner
Ertzney / Jhe schwerer die schmertze ist / jhe Sorgfeltiger Gott ist fur
vnser gesundheit / Vnd ob er wol droben im Himel sitzet / so sihet
er doch jnn die tieffe / Wir sollen nicht klagen / das die kranckheit zu
lange were / vnd das die schmertze zu gros sey / Denn Gott ist getrew
/ der vns nicht lesset versuchen / vber vnser vermu[e]gen / Lassen wir
vns du[e]ncken / wir fu[e]len kei-[C6r] ne hu[e]lff noch trost eusserlich
am leibe / So sollen wir vns des versehen / das wir die hu[e]lffe reichlich
fu[e]len werden an der Seelen. Wir sollen gewislich gleuben / das Gott
die hu[e]lffe nicht verzeucht / als wolt er vns nicht helffen / sondern
allein darumb / das er sie zu seiner zeit / viel herrlicher vnd tro[e]stlicher
erzeige / mehr denn wir hetten du[e]rffen hoffen vnd wu[e]ndschen.
Es heisset / wie man singt / Die hoffnung wart der rechten zeit / was
Gottes Wort zusaget / Wenn das geschehen sol zur freud / setzt Gott
kein gewisse tage / Er weis wol wenns am besten ist / vnd braucht an
vns kein arge list / das sollen wir jm vertrawen. Ob sichs an lies als wolt
er nicht / Las dich es nicht erschrecken / Denn wo er ist am besten mit
/ da wil ers nicht entdecken / Sein Wort las dir gewisser sein / vnd ob
dein hertz sprech lauter nein / so las dir doch nicht grawen.

confidence. He will not abandon me in any distress, nor will he place me under his eternal condemnation. Therefore, I cry with most ardent desire to him, just as Christ (to give me a comforting example) did on the cross, 'O God, heavenly Father, come help me in my final distress. Into you hands I commend my spirit [Luke 23:46]. Amen.'"

Give me a short form, how I should admonish a dying person to be patient and to surrender to God's will.

First of all, say, "Dear friend, remember that you have not come into this world in order to remain here (that would be to remain in misery) but rather so that (when God wills that you should lay aside the trouble and toil of this miserable life through temporal death) you do not concern yourself further with this world's blessings, which pass away, but with lofty heavenly things, indeed, with the highest blessing, which is God himself. That cannot fully happen unless the Old Adam dies. This death is shared by you and all people. For, as we have all sinned in Adam, we must all therefore suffer and bear the punishment of sin, death. The greater the illness, the nearer is God with his remedy; the worse the pains, the more solicitous God is for our health. Even though he is sitting up there in heaven, he sees into the depths. We should not complain that the illness is too long and that the pains too bad. For God is faithful. He will not let us be put to the test beyond our ability [to bear it][1 Cor. 10:13]. If we think that we feel no help or comfort outwardly in the body, we should see to it that we feel his help richly in the soul. We should certainly believe that God does not withdraw his help from us as if he did not want to help, but only so that in his own time he can show us in much more glorious and comforting fashion even more than we would have been able to hope for and desire. That means, as we sing, "hope waits for what God's Word has promised the right time, when it is to take place for our joy. God does not set specific days [for our death]. He knows when it is best, and he does not deceive us: that much confidence we can have in him. Even if it appears that it is not his will, do not be terrified. For he does not want to let us know where he is with us for our greatest advantage. Let his Word be sure for you, and even if your heart says nothing but 'no,' don't let it fill you with horror."[33]
Second.

---

33   The eleventh and twelfth stanzas of the hymn "Ein Lied vom Gesetz und Glauben," more familiarly known as "Es ist das hey vns kommen her" ("Salvation

[C6v] Zum andern.

Sprich / Lieber Mensch / Du weist das du sterben solt vnd must / vnd ist kein ander Weg zum Himlischen Vater / denn durch den zeitlichen Tod. Darumb wende dich willig von allen Creaturen / Weib / kindern / freunden / gu[e]tern / vnd aller welt / vnd kere dich allein zu Gott / Denn er kan dir allein auff diesem engen Wege hindurch helffen. Gedenck an den spruch Christi Joh. 16 Ein Weib / wenn sie gebirt / ist sie traurig / Wenn sie aber das kind geboren hat / gedenckt sie der angst nicht mehr / Also thu jhm auch. Gedulde / leid vnd schweig / ergreiff die hoffnung / Gedenck / es sey vmb ein sprung zu thun / so wirds besser werden / vnd wird folgen eitel fried / freude / vnd ewiges Leben / Amen.

Zum dritten.

Sprich / Lieber Mensch / gedenck [C7r] an deine Tauff / denn darzu bistu getaufft / das du sterben solt vnd must. Da hastu Brieff vnd Sigil / das dein leiden vnd Tod / Christus Leiden vnd Tod ist. Du hast in der Tauffe gewisse zeichen vnd versicherung empfangen / das du im sterben / dem Teuffel / Tod / Su[e]nd vnd Helle / im Namen Christi / solt obsiegen / vnd am Ju[e]ngsten Tage wider auffstehen von den Todten / vnd ewiglich leben. Gleich wie Christus vnser lieber HERR / durch sein Leiden vnd sterben / Teuffel / Tod / Su[e]nd vnd Helle vberwunden hat / vnd ist von den Todten aufferstanden / vnd lebet ewiglich / Darzu soltu dich auch tro[e]sten / das dieser dein leiblicher abschied von dieser Welt / wird dir nicht ein schmertzlich sterben noch tod sein / sondern ein Schlaff vnd Friedfart / vnd selige Hinfart / ein beschliessen aller angst vn kranckheit / Ein pfort [C7v] vnd Eingang zum ewigen Leben. Gedenck auch / das Gott Vater / Son / vnd der Heilige Geist (in welcher Namen du getaufft bist) dir versprochen haben / bey dir vnd mit dir / zu sein vnd bleiben / in allerley anfechtung / angst vnd not / ja fur dich zu kempffen vnd zu streiten / widder alle deine Feinde / vnd dich entlich durch Tod / Su[e]nde / vnd Helle / hindurch bringen / zum ewigen Leben.

Zum vierden.

Sprich also / Lieber Mensch / Wollen dich deine manchfeltigen su[e]nde anfechten vnd beku[e]mmern / So nim dich dismal / deiner su[e]nde nicht an / Sondern opffer sie dem ho[e]chsten Priester / Christo / auff sein Creutz / mit einem Rewigem hertzen / vnd betru[e]btem

Say, "Dear friend, you know that you are supposed to die and that you must die, and there is no other way to the heavenly Father than through temporal death. Therefore, turn yourself willingly away from all creatures, wife, children, friends, property, and all the world, and turn yourself to God alone. For only he can help you on this narrow path to the end. Remember the words of Christ, John 16 [:21], 'When a woman is in labor, she is miserable, but when the child is born, she no longer remembers the anguish.' Do the same thing. Be patient, suffer and be silent. Grasp the hope. Remember that with one leap it will be better, and nothing but peace, joy, and eternal life will be the result. Amen."

Third.

Say, "Dear friend, think of your baptism. For you have been baptized because you are supposed to die and must die. In your baptism you have a promise signed and sealed that your suffering and death is Christ's suffering and death. You have received in your baptism a sure sign and guarantee, so that in your death you will triumph over the devil, death, sin and hell in the name of Christ and so that you will rise from the dead on the Last Day and live forever, just as Christ our dear Lord, has conquered the devil, death, sin, and hell through his suffering and death and is risen from the dead and lives eternally. For this reason you should find comfort, that your physical departure from this world will not be a painful dying or death for you but rather a sleep and a peaceful journey and a blessed departure, the ending of all fears and illness, a gate and entrance to eternal life. Remember also that God, Father, Son, and Holy Spirit (in whose name you are baptized), has promised you to be and remain next to you—with you in all temptations, fears, and misery—and to fight and battle in your behalf against all these enemies, and bring you finally through death, sin, and hell, to eternal life."

Fourth.

Say, "Dear friend, if your many sins are trying to assault you and make you worry, just do not accept your sins as your own this time, but with a remorseful heart and grieving spirit offer them to the High

Unto Us Has Come") by Paul Speratus (1484-1551) Wackernagel, *Kirchenlied* 3:32).

Geiste / vnd vertrawe auff seine gu[e]te vnd barm- [C8r] hertzigkeit.
Gedenck / das vns Gott der Vater / so hertzlich geliebet hat / das er
auch seinen Einigen Son / der nie keine Su[e]nde gethan hat / Fur vns
gegeben hat / auff das wir jnn jhm wu[e]rden die Gerechtigkeit / die
fur Gott gilt / Schu[e]tte deine Su[e]nde auff das Lamb Gottes / auff
Jhesum Christum / der der Welt Su[e]nde tregt / Gedenck / das er vns
gemacht ist / zur Gerechtigkeit / zur Heiligung / vnd zur Erlo[e]sung
/ das Er Dir / vnd aller welt zu trost / geboren ist / dir gestorben / vnd
am Creutz vnter die Vbeltheter gerechet / dir aufferstanden / Vnd /
wie er deine Su[e]nde / durch seinen Tod / ausgetilget hat / vnd alle
deine Feinde vberwunden / Also hat er dir solchen Triumph vnd Sieg
/ auch geschenckt / Gleub du nur / vnd halt dich an sein Wort / das
wird dir [C8v] nicht feilen / Er hat gesagt / Wer an den Son Gottes
gleubt / der hat das ewige Leben. Gleubstu das? So ko[e]mpstu nicht
jns Gerichte der verdampten / Sondern du wirst gehen durch den
zeitlichen Tod / in das ewige Leben.

   Zum fu[e]nfften.
   Sprich / Lieber Mensch / Wil dich der Teuffel mit Gottes zorn / vnd
mit der Hellischen pein schrecken / Las dichs nicht anfechten / Stehe
nur fest im glauben / Denn deine seligkeit ist gebawet auff den starcken
Felsen / Christum / Dem mu[e]ssen alle Hellische pforten weichen /
Warumb woltestu dich auff diesem Wege fu[e]rchten? Jst doch Gott
mit dir / vnd bey dir. Warumb woltestu auch den Tod fu[e]rchten?
Thut er dir doch die Thu[e]r auff / zu dem ewigen Leben. [D1r] Las
die vngleubigen vnd Gottlose menschen den Tod fu[e]rchten / die durch
den zeitlichen Tod gehen zu dem ewigen Tod. Las die fur dem Tod
erschrecken / die Christum nicht zum Heiland haben. Las den Reichen
Man sich fur dem Tode fu[e]rchten / denn der mus in die Helle. Du
aber frewe dich / Denn heute wirstu mit dem armen Lazaro im schos
Abrahe / die ewige Ruge empfahen. Bis getrost / Heute wirstu mit
Christo vnd dem Schecher im Paradise / ewige lust vnd freude haben.
Jtzund ru[e]fft dir Christus / vnd spricht / Nu kom zu mir / Heute
wil ich deine mu[e]he / last vnd arbeit / von dir nemen / vnd dich mit
ewiger freude erquicken.

   Zum sechsten.
   Sprich / Lieber Mensch / Erinnere dich auch / das du em- [D1v]
pfangen hast / das Pfand der Gnaden / das hochwirdige Sacrament

Priest, Christ, who is on his cross, and trust in his goodness and mercy. Remember that God the Father loved us so fervently that he gave his only Son, who had committed no sin, for us, so that we might become in him the righteousness that avails in God's sight. Pour out your sin on the lamb of God, on Jesus Christ, who bears the sins of the world [John 1:29]. Remember that he has been made our righteousness, sanctification, and redemption [1 Cor. 1:30]. Remember that he was born to be your consolation and the consolation of the whole world, that he died for you and on the cross was counted among the criminals for you, that he rose for you. As he blotted out your sins through his death and conquered all your enemies, so he has given you the gift of this triumph and victory. Just believe. Cling to his Word. It will not fail you. He has said, 'Whoever believes in the Son of God has everlasting life' [John 3:16]. Do you believe that? If you do, you will not come into the judgment of the condemned, but you will go through temporal death into eternal life."

Fifth.

Say, "Dear friend, when the devil wants to terrify you with God's wrath and the torment of hell, do not let yourself be assaulted. Stand steadfast in faith! For your salvation is built upon the strong rock, Christ, and the gates of hell must give way before him. Why do you want to be afraid on this path? God is indeed with you and alongside you. Why do you want to fear death? Death opens the door for you to eternal life. Let the unbelievers and godless fear death; they pass through temporal death into eternal death. Let those who do not have Christ as savior be afraid in the face of death. Let the rich man be afraid in the face of death since he must go to hell. But you, rejoice! since today you will receive eternal rest with poor Lazarus in Abraham's bosom [Luke 16:19-31]. Take comfort! Today you will have eternal pleasure and joy with Christ and with the thief from the cross in Paradise [Luke 23:39-43]. Now Christ is calling to you and says, 'Come to me. Today I will take your troubles, burden, and labor from you and refresh you with eternal joy'" [Matt. 22:28].

Sixth.

den Fronleichnam Jhesu Christi / der fur dich am Creutz gestorben ist
/ vnd hast getruncken sein theures blut / das er zur vergebung deiner
su[e]nde vergossen hat / auff das du deiner su[e]nde frey / ledig vnd los
wu[e]rdest / Der frome CHristus hat sich gedemu[e]tiget vnd ernidriget
/ ist zu dir komen / vnd ist beide dein Wirt vnd Gast worden / Er hat
dich gespeiset mit seinem Heiligen Leibe / fur den ewigen Hunger /
vnd dich getrenckt mit seinem theuren Blute / fur den ewigen Durst /
vnd hat (Jhm zur Wonunge vnd Herberge) deine Seele erwelet / auff
das Er fur dich sorge / fur dich kempffe vnd streite / das dir kein Feind
noch Vnfall / schaden mu[e]ge / vnd du auff diesem Wege / keinen
mangel leidest / sondern jnn Gottes schutz vnd hu- [D2r] te / durch
die lieben Engel / getragen werdest in das ewige Leben.

Zum siebenden.
Sprich / Nu far hin lieber Mensch / far hin in Gottes friede / Zweiuel
nicht an Gottes Zusagen. Denn Gott hat dir das ewige Leben versprochen / des wird er dir nicht entpfallen. Er ist warhafftig / So ist dis dein
sterben / ein selige Hinfart / aus diesem mu[e]hesamen Leben / in das
ewige Leben. Erinnere dich der Worte deines Heilmachers Christi / da
er sagt / Johan. am 14. Jch bin der Weg / die Warheit / vnd das Leben.
Volge Christo / so kanstu nicht irren / Denn Er ist der Weg. Gleube
Christo / so kanstu nicht betrogen werden / Denn Er ist die Warheit.
Bleib in Christo / so kanstu nicht des ewigen Tods sterben / Denn er
[D2v] ist das Leben. Darumb / Lieber Mensch / Ergib dich willig /
mit allem das du bist vnd vermagst / deinem Schepffer / Opffere dich
Gott dem Vater / mit leib vnd seele / zu einem lebendigen / heiligen
/ vnd wolgefelligen Opffer / vnd sprich / mit deinem Erlo[e]ser Jhesu
Christo / O Vater / in deine hende befehle ich meinen Geist.
    Nu Lieber bruder / Liebe schwester / Der Almechtige / ewige /
barmhertzige Gott / beleite dich in das ewige Leben / vnd verleihe dir
eine fro[e]liche Aufferstehung am Ju[e]ngsten Gerichte / vnd darnach
die ewigen Seligkeit / Amen.

Ein Gebetlin / bey dem sterbenden Menschen.
O HERR Jhesu Christ / du einiger Son des Himelischen Vaters /
vnser Erlo[e]ser / Heiland / vnd [D3r] Seligmacher / Wir bitten dich
/ Erlo[e]se diesen sterbenden Menschen / von allen grewlichen / vnd
erschrecklichen Bilden vnd anfechtungen des Teuffels / der Su[e]nden
/ vnd der Helle. Erlo[e]se jhn / wie du gnediglich erlo[e]set hast Noe

Say, "Dear friend, remember that you have received the guarantee of grace, the holy sacrament of the body of Jesus Christ, who died for you on the cross, and you have drunk his precious blood, that he poured out for the forgiveness of your sins, so that you would be free, released, and liberated from your sins. Christ, who is ever faithful, humbled and humiliated himself and has come to you. He is both host and guest. He has fed you with his holy body for the eternal hunger, and he has given you to drink of his precious blood for the eternal thirst. He has chosen your soul as his dwelling place and lodging so that he can care for you, can do battle and fight for you, so that no foe nor misfortune can harm you and so that you lack nothing on your way but that in God's protection and care you will be carried by the holy angels into eternal life."

Seventh.
Say, "Depart, dear friend, depart in God's peace. Do not doubt God's assurance. For God has given you his promise, and he will not forget this promise to you. He is faithful. Therefore, this death that you are dying is a blessed departure out of this wearisome life into eternal life. Remember the words of your Savior Christ when he said, John 14 [:6], 'I am the way, the truth, and the life.' Follow Christ, and you cannot go astray. For he is the way. Believe in Christ, and you cannot be deceived. For he is the truth. Remain in Christ, and you cannot die the eternal death. For he is the life. Therefore, dear friend, willingly turn yourself over to your Creator with all that you are and all that you are able to do. Offer yourself to God the Father, with body and soul, as a living, holy, pleasing sacrifice, and say with your Redeemer, Jesus Christ, 'O Father, into your hands I commend my spirit'" [Luke 23:46].

"Dear brother, dear sister, the Almighty, eternal, merciful God accompany you into eternal life and grant you a joyous resurrection at the Last Judgment and thereafter eternal bliss. Amen."

A Short prayer for a dying person.
O Lord Jesus Christ, only Son of the Heavenly Father, our Redeemer, Deliverer, and Savior, we entreat you, deliver this dying person from all

von den Bu[e]lgen der Sindflut. Loth / von dem verderben Sodome.
Abraham / vom dem Fewer der Chaldeer. Die kinder Jsrael / von der
gewalt Pharaonis. David / von der hand Goliath. Die drey Menner /
von dem Feuroffen Babilonis. Daniel / aus der Lewen gruben. Jonam /
aus dem Bauch des Walfisches. Petrum / aus dem Gefengnis Herodis.
Also erlo[e]se auch / O HErr Gott / die Seele dieses sterbenden Menschen / von aller ferligkeit / Ero[e]ffene ihm heut zu tage / die Thu[e]r
des Paradises / die Pforten des Himels / vnd den Eingang des [D3v]
ewigen Lebens. O HErr Christe / verzeihe jhm alle seine Su[e]nde /
vnd fu[e]re jhn mit freuden jnn das Reich deines Himlischen Vaters
/ jnn den Schos Abrahe / zu ewiger Ruge / auff das er mit dir / vnd
allen auserwelten Kindern Gottes / on ende sich frewe / im ewigen
leben / Amen.

Ein ander Gebet.
O Almechtiger / ewiger Gott / der du erleuchtest alle Menschen / die
da komen in diese Welt / Wir bitten dich / erleuchte das hertz dieses
krancken / mit dem glantze deiner Go[e]ttlichen gnade / auff das alle
seine gedancken / wort vnd wercke / dahin geordenet vnd gerichtet
sein / das er im Glauben / vnd in der Liebe / deiner Go[e]ttlichen
Maiestat gefellig werde / durch Jhesum Christum deinen Son / vnsern
HErrn / Amen.

[D4r] Ein ander Gebet.
O gu[e]tiger / barmhertziger Gott / du einiges Heil vnd trost aller
gleubigen / Erho[e]re vns vber diesen deinen krancken Diener / da
vor wir deine Go[e]ttliche hu[e]lffe anruffen / Verleihe jm widderumb
sein gesundheit / auff das er dir / in Christlicher Gemeine dancksage
allezeit / durch Jhesum Christum / Amen.

Ein anders.
O barmhertziger Gott / der du deinem Diener Ezechie / sein leben
verlenget / vnd funffzehen jar zugelegt hast / Wir bitten dich / wollest
diesen deinen Diener / von dem bette der schmertzen vnd Kranckheit /
durch deine Go[e]ttliche gewalt / widerumb auffheben zur Gesundheit
/ durch JHesum CHristum / Amen.

dreadful, terrifying machinations and assaults of the devil, of sin, and of hell. Deliver him, as you graciously redeemed Noah from the billows of the Flood [Gen. 6:9-9:17], Lot from the corruption of Sodom [Gen. 18:16-19:29], Abraham from the fire of the Chaldeans [based on a misreading of Gen. 15:7],[34] the children of Israel from the power of Pharaoh [Ex. 5:1-15:27], David from the hand of Goliath [1 Sam. 17:1-58], the three men from the fiery furnace of Babylon [Dan. 3:1-30], Daniel from the lion's den [Dan. 6:1-28], Jonah from the belly of the whale [Jon. 1:1-2:10], Peter from Herod's prison [Acts 12:1-19]. Deliver, O Lord God, the soul of this dying person from all dangers. Open to him this very day the gates of paradise, the portals of heaven, and the entrance to eternal life. O Lord Christ, pardon him all his sins and lead him with joy into the realm of your heavenly Father, into Abraham's bosom, to eternal rest, so that he may rejoice unceasingly with you and all the chosen children of God in eternal life. Amen.

Another prayer.

O almighty, eternal God, you enlighten all people who come into this world. We ask you, enlighten the heart of the sick person with the splendor of your divine grace, that all his thoughts, words, and deeds, may be ordered and directed to pleasing the divine majesty in faith and in love, through Jesus Christ, your Son, our Lord. Amen.

Another prayer.

O good and merciful God, you who are the only salvation and consolation of all believers, hear our prayer for your servant who is ill. [Even] before we appeal to your divine help, grant him health once again, that he may at all times give you thanks in the congregation of Christians, through Jesus Christ. Amen.

One more.

O merciful God, who lengthened the life of your servant Hezekiah and added fifteen years [to his life] [2 Kings 10:1-11], we pray you

---

34   In Genesis 15:7 God is cited as saying to Abraham, "I am the Lord, who brought you out of Ur of the Chaldeans ... ." The Hebrew word for "fire," "Or," was substituted for "Ur" in the text by rabbinic sources based upon the first-century Targum of Jonathon ben-Uzziel, a disciple of Hillel. The midrash on the text conveyed a story of Abraham's deliverance to Christian medieval biblical comment.

[D4v] Ein ander Gebet.

O Almechtiger Vater / wir bitten dich / Sihe auff diesen deinen Diener / der da inn kranckheit seines leibs hernider ligt / Erquicke seine Seele / die du geschaffen hast / Auff das / so er durch leibliche straffe / versucht vnd gereiniget / bald befinde / sich durch deine barmhertzigkeit / von allem Wehe entlediget / durch Jhesum Christum / Amen.

Ein anders.

O Ewiger / Barmhertziger Gott / Sihe herab von Himel / besuche diesen deinen krancken Diener / wie du besucht hast Thobiam vnd Saram. Die schwieger Petri / vnd den knecht Centurionis. Gesegene jn / wie du gesegenet hast Abraham / Jsaac / vnd Jacob. Sihe jhn an HERR Gott mit den [D5r] augen deiner barmhertzigkeit / Erfu[e]lle jhn mit aller freude / vnd treib von jm alle su[e]ndliche begirde / Vnd sende herab deinen Engel des friedes / das er jn erhalte vnd schu[e]tze / in ewigem Friede / durch Jhesum CHhristum deinen Son / vnsern HERRN / Amen.

Hie befihl den krancken / Gott dem Almechtigen / vnd sprich.

Heile dich Gott der Vater / der dich geschaffen hat. Helffe dir Gott der Son / der dich erlo[e]set hat. Stercke dich der Heilige Geist / der dir in der Tauff gegeben ist. Erhalte dich dein Glaube / der dich von allen su[e]nden erlediget hat / Amen.

Gesegene dich Gott der Vater. Behu[e]te dich der HErr Christus. Erleuchte dich der Heilige Geist. Bestetige dich die Krafft Gottes / vnd vergebe dir alle deine Su[e]nde / Amen.

[D5v] Der Segen / Schutz vnd Heilmachung des almechtigen Vaters / vnd des Sons / vnd des Heiligen Geistes / kome vber dich / vnd behu[e]te dich fur allem vbel / vnd fu[e]re dich entlich zum ewigen Leben / Amen.

that you will raise up your servant from this bed of pain and illness
through your divine power to health, through Jesus Christ. Amen.

Another prayer.

O Almighty Father, we beseech you, look upon this your servant, who
has been laid low by physicial illness. Quicken his soul, which you have
created, so that, tried and purified through bodily affliction, he will find
himself quickly delivered from all travail through your mercy, through
Jesus Christ. Amen

Another.

O eternal, merciful God, look down from heaven and visit this your
servant, who is ill, as you visited Tobias and Sarah [Tob. 3:1-22:20], the
mother-in-law of Peter [Matt. 8:1-15] and the servant of the Centurion
[Luke 7:1-10]. Bless him as you blessed Abraham, Isaac, and Jacob. Look
at him, Lord God, with the eyes of your mercy. Fill him with all joy,
and drive out of him all sinful desires. Send down your angel of peace
that he may be preserved and protected in eternal peace, through Jesus
Christ, your Son, our Lord. Amen

At this point commend the sick to God the Almighty and say

May God the Father, who has created you, heal you. May God the
Son, who has redeemed you, help you. May God the Holy Spirit, who
was given to you in your baptism, strengthen you. May your faith, which
has taken care of all your sins, preserve you. Amen

May God the Father bless you. May the Lord Christ protect you.
May the Holy Spirit enlighten you. May the power of God strengthen
you and forgive you all your sins. Amen.

Pio Lectori.
Ad Stiga delictis, virtutibus itur ad astra.
Saluus erit summam, qui perseuerat in horam.

May the blessing, protection, and salvation of the almighty Father, the Son, and the Holy Spirit come upon you and protect you in the face of all evil, and lead you finally to eternal life. Amen

Pio Lectori.
Ad Stiga delictis, virtutibus itur ad astra.
Saluus erit summam, qui perseuerat in horam.

[D6r] VOM CHRISTLICHEN RITTER:

MIT WAS FEINDEN ER KEMPFFEN MUS.

EIN KURTZER VNTERRICHT /
AUS DER HEILIGEN SCHRIFFT /

DURCH /
M. JOHAN. SPANGENBERG.
1548.

[D6V BLANK]

ON THE CHRISTIAN KNIGHT
AND THE ENEMIES WITH WHICH HE MUST FIGHT
A BRIEF INSTRUCTION FROM HOLY SCRIPTURE,

BY
JOHANN SPANGENBERG
1548

[D7r] Den Erbarn / vorsichtigen vnd weisen Herrn / Er Wolff Pucher / Hans Stalh / Jacob Heidelberg / vnd Christoffel Mosshawer / Meinen gu[e]nstigen lieben Patronen / herren vnd freunden.

Gnad vnd Fried durch Christum vnsern Herrn. Nach dem der Almechtige / ewige Barmhertzige Gott / der lo[e]blichen Herrschafft Manssfeld / eine sonderliche gnade fur andern / verliehen hat / nicht allein mit dem vnausschepfflichen Bergwerck begnad / sondern auch in derselbigen / einen Man / erweckt / der die rechten Himlischen Fundgruben ero[e]ffnet / ein Ewig / Selig Berckwerck des Go[e]ttlichen Worts angericht hat // Aus welches Schechten vnd Stollen / nichts [D7v] anders / denn Himlisch Ertz / vnd quelle des lebendigen Wassers / geschepfft werden / Habt jr jnn genanter Herrschafft Gott dem Almechtigen viel zu dancken / je ernstlich zu bitten / das er solches seligen Berckwercks Adern vnd Genge / beide leiblich vnd geistlich / jm lasse befohlen sein / vnd zu gedeien aller Landsassen / gnediglichen erhalte. Weil aber auch der Teuffel / Gottes gaben mechtig feind ist / vnd mit allem vleis darnach erbeitet / das er euch derselbigen beraube / odder ja verhindere / vnd an leib vnd seel verderbe / Jst euch zum schutz / widder einen solchen Feind / guter wehr vnd waffen wol von no[e]ten / Damit jr nu den rechten Harnisch Gottes mu[e]get ergreiffen / vnd wider den Teuffel Ritterlich fechten / hab ich mir / neben meinen geschefften / so viel zeit vnd weile genomen / dis Bu[e]chlin / vom Christlichen Rit- [D8r] ter zusamen bracht / vnd euch (als von denen ich viel guts empfangen) dedicirt vnd zugeschrieben / Darinnen angezeigt / Was ein Christlicher Ritter sey / Worinne die Christliche Ritterschafft stehe / vnd was er fur Waffen brauchen mus / damit er widder den Heubtfeind den Teuffel / Ritterlich mu[e]ge fechten / auch den Sieg behalten / Bitte demu[e]tiglich / jr

To the honorable, prudent, wise gentlemen, Wolff
Pucher, Hans Stahl, Jacob Heidelberg, and Chris-
topher Mosshauer,[35] my gracious dear patrons,
lords, and friends.

Grace and peace from Christ our Lord. The Almighty, eternal,
merciful God has bestowed upon the praiseworthy principality
of Mansfeld a special grace beyond that of other lands. He not
only graced it with inexhaustible mines but also, with this same grace,
raised up a man who opened up the true heavenly lode and established
an eternal, salvific mine of the divine Word. Out of its shafts and tunnels are drawn nothing other than heavenly ore and a fountain of living
water.[36] Therefore, you in your principality have much for which to give
the Almighty thanks, and have [good reason] to pray fervently that he
let you place these veins and tunnels, both physical and spiritual, in his
hands, and to pray that he graciously preserve them for the well-being
of all inhabitants of the land. However, the devil is dead set against
God's gifts and is working very diligently to rob you of these gifts or at
least prevent you from enjoying them. [He is working very diligently]
to cause you both physical and spiritual ruin. Because of this it is necessary for you to have as protection against such a foe a good defense and
weaponry, so that you may grasp the real armor of God and valiantly
fight against the devil. Therefore, in addition to my other activities I
have taken time to assemble this booklet on the Christian knight, and
I am dedicating and addressing it to you (because I have received so
much good from you). In this booklet is shown what a Christian knight
is, in what Christian knighthood consists, and what kind of weapons a
Christian knight must use to fight against the chief enemy, the devil, in
gallant fashion and to win the victory. I ask in humility that you kindly

---

35   These four men were apparently civic leaders in Mansfeld.

36   Martin Luther had been born in Mansfeld county, in the village of Eisleben,
in 1483 and had grown up in the town of Mansfeld. Johann Spangenberg's
son Cyriakus used the mining motif in some of the sermons he preached on
Luther and his proclamation in a series finally published as *Luther, Man of
God* (*Theander Luther. Von des werten Gottes Manne Doctor Martin Luthers
Geistliche Haushaltung ...* [Ursel: Nikolaus Heinrich, 1589]), in which Luther
also is dealt with in one sermon as a "knight of God."

wollet diese kleine verehrung / zum seligen newen jare / freundlich
annemen / Christus vnser lieber HEJland / wo[e]lle euch / sampt
ewern lieben Hausfrawen / Kindern vnd Gesinde / in reiner Lere des
Euangelij / allezeit gnediglich erhalten. Datum Northausen Anno /
1541. am Sontag nach Epiphanie.

E. W. V.
M. Johan. Spangenberg.

accept this small honor for a blessed new year. May Christ our dear Savior preserve you, with your dear wives, children, and servants, for all time in the pure teaching of the gospel. Given at Nordhausen, on the Sunday after Epiphany 1541.

Your Worthinesses' servant,[37] E.W.V.
M. Johann Spangenberg

---

37   The abbreiviation "E.W.V." is used here and stands for "Ewer Erwirden Vntertheniger."

[D8v] Was ist ein Christliche Ritter?

EJn Christlicher Ritter / ist ein Gleubiger Mensch / der jnn der Tauff / durch wasser vnd Geist new geboren ist / Hat einen rechten Glauben / gewisse Hoffnung / vnd warhafftige Liebe / zu Gott vnd dem Nehisten / Helt an reiner Euangelischer Lere / vnd ist bereit / allezeit zu kempffen / vnd zu streiten / wider den Teuffel / Welt / vnd sein Eigen Fleisch / vnd was jm daru[e]ber begegend / dasselbige mit gedult leidet vnd tregt / vmb Gottes willen.

Worinne stehet die Christliche Ritterschafft?

Jnn dreien dingen / Nemlich / 1 Jnn der verleuckung des Teuffels / der Welt / vnd des Eigenen fleisches. [E1r] 2 Jnn der vbung des glaubens gegen Gott / vnd der Liebe gegen dem Nehisten. 3 Jnn der to[e]dtung des alten Adams / des su[e]ndlichen Fleisches / vnd newerung des Geistes / gegen jm selbs.

Wo vermanet vns die Schrifft / zur verleuckung des Teuffels?

Also sagt S. Jacob in seiner Epistelam [!] 4. Capitel / Seid Gott vnterthenig / Widderstehet dem Teuffel / so fleuhet er von euch / Nahet euch zu Gott / so nahet er sich zu euch.

Was ist der Teuffel fur ein ding?

Der Teuffel ist anfenglich von Gott nicht bo[e]se geschaffen / Sondern ist aus eigner bosheit gefallen / wie Christus sagt Johan. am 8. Er ist in der warheit nicht bestanden.

[E1v] Wie wird der Teuffel genennet?

Christus nennet in Johan. 8. einen Mordgeist vnd Lu[e]gengeist / Denn er stehet dem Menschen nach leib vnd seele / Den leib zu to[e]dten / mit Fewr / Wasser / Schwerd / Pestilentz etc. Die seele / mit falscher Lere / lu[e]gen vnd jrthumb / Denn also sagt Christus / Er ist ein Mo[e]rder von anfang / vnd ist nicht bestanden jnn der Warheit / Wenn er die lu[e]gen redet / so redet er von seinem eigen / Denn er ist ein Lu[e]gener / vnd ein Vater derselbigen / Er ist ein Feind des Lebens vnd der Warheit / vnd ist jm leid / das ein Mensch sol selig werden / vnd an den ort komen / daraus er verstossen ist.

Er heisset auch Sathan / Diabolus / ein Lesterer / Verleumbder / Ankleger / das er Gottes Wort Le- [E2r] stert / taddelt / vnd auffs ergste

What is a Christian knight?

A Christian knight is a believer, who has been born anew in baptism through water and the Spirit [John 3:5], has a true faith, a certain hope, and genuine love [1 Cor. 13:13] for God and the neighbor, holds to pure evangelical teaching, and is prepared to fight and to struggle at all times against the devil, the world, and his own flesh. He suffers and bears whatever he encounters with patience for the sake of God.

In what does Christian knighthood consist?

In three things, namely (1) in the denial of the devil, the world, and the flesh, (2) in the exercise of faith in God and love for the neighbor, and (3) in the killing of the old Adam, the sinful flesh, and the renewal of the spirit within a person's own life.

Where does Scripture admonish us to deny the devil?

Saint James says in his epistle, chapter four [Jas. 4:7-8]: "Submit to God. Resist the devil, and he will flee before you. Come close to God."

What sort of thing is the devil?

The devil was not originally created evil by God but fell due to his own wickedness, as Christ says, John 8 [:44], "He does not stand in the truth."

What names are ascribed to the devil?

In John 8 [:44] Christ labels him a murderous spirit and a deceiving spirit, for he is after the human being in body and soul, to kill the body with fire, water, sword, plague, etc., and to kill the soul with false teaching, deception, and error. For Christ says, "He was a murderer from the beginning and does not stand in the truth. When he lies, he speaks according to his own nature, for he is a liar and the father of lies." He is an enemy of life and truth, and he hates it when a human being is saved and goes to the place from which he [the devil] was expelled.

He is called Satan, Diabolus, a slanderer, a defamer, an accuser, because he misrepresents and finds fault with God's Word and twists it

verkeret / wie er Heua / im Paradis thet / Gene. 3. Er verklaget Gottes
Kinder / tag vnd nacht fur Gott / Apo. 12. Er ist auch ein Verterber /
vnterstehet sich / alle Gottes ordenung / alle Policey / alle Haushaltung
/ allen rechten Gottes dienst / zu hindern vnd zu verterben / Hetzet
Ju[e]den / Tu[e]rcken / Heiden / Tyrannen an die Christen / macht
vnfried / Entzu[e]ndet die vnruigen hertzen / erweckt Auffrhur vnd
Empo[e]rung / Treibt die falschen Lerer das sie Rotten vnd Secten
anrichten / Vergifftet die Lufft / verterbet die Fru[e]chte auff dem felde
/ Fu[e]ret die Menschen jnn alle vntugent / su[e]nd vnd laster / Er ist
vnser Widdersacher / gehet vmbher wie ein bru[e]llender Lewe / vnd
suchet / welchen er verschlinge. 1. Petri 5.

[E2v] Wo hat der Teuffel sein wonung?
S. Paulus Ephe. 6. schreibt also / Wir haben nicht mit fleisch vnd
blut zu kempffen / sondern mit Fu[e]rsten vnd Gewaltigen / Nemlich
/ mit den Herrn der Welt / die in der finsternis dieser Welt herrschen.
Da nennet er sie Cosmocratores / Fu[e]rsten der Welt / Bo[e]se Geister / die in der Lufft regiren / Schweben vber vns / wie die wolcken /
Fladdern allenthalben vmb vns / wie Hummeln / mit grossen hauffen /
Lassen sich offt jnn leiblicher gestalt sehen / vnd sind gerne an wu[e]sten
o[e]rten / Heusern vnd Wildnussen.

So ho[e]re ich wol / der Teuffel ist noch nicht zur Helle verstossen?
Also sagt S. Petrus 2. Petri 2 Gott hat sie mit ketten der Finsternis /
zur Helle vbergeben / das sie [E3r] zum Gericht behalten werden / Jnn
des haben sie jnne die Lufft / vnd alles was vber vns ist / Da sitzen vnd
schweben sie / sehen vnd lauren auff vns / wie sie vns nur schaden thun
/ vnd an leib vnd seel verterben / Er ist ein Doctor in aller schalckheit /
hat grosse erfarung / weis gar wol / wo er einen jglichen sol angreiffen.
Wir du[e]rffen auch nicht dencken / das er weit von vns ist / jrgend
jnn Jndia / Aphrica / odder in Morenland / sondern er ist hart bey vns

in the worst possible ways, as he did with Eve in Paradise, Genesis 3 [:1-19]. He lodges accusations before God against God's children day and night, Revelation 12 [:9]. He trashes things, and he impudently strives to obstruct and subvert God's design for the world, all law and order, all family life, all proper worship. He arouses the Jews, Turks, pagans, and tyrants against the Christians, causes discord, enflames restless hearts, provokes rebellion and revolt, impels teachers to organize factions and sects, poisons the air, makes the fruits of the fields spoil, leads people into every vice, sin, and wickedness. He is our adversary and prowls about like a roaring lion, looking for someone to devour, 1 Peter 5 [:8].

Where does the devil dwell?

Saint Paul writes in Ephesians 6 [:12], "Our struggle is not against enemies of flesh and blood, but against the rulers, against the authorities, namely against the lords of his world, who rule in the darkness of this world." There he names these "comsocratores,"[38] these princes of the world, evil spirits who rule in the air. They float over us like clouds, buzz around us on every side like bumblebees, in a large swarm; they often appear in physical form, and they like deserted places, deserted houses, and wilderness.

So I guess I am hearing that the devil has not yet been thrown into hell?

Saint Peter says, 2 Peter 2 [:4], that God has cast them into hell in the chains of darkness. There they are to be held until the Judgment. For the time being they are occupying the air and everything that is above us. There they sit, posed in the air, and they watch us and observe us, [contemplating] how they can do us harm and bring ruin upon us in body and soul. He [the devil] is a doctor[39] of every kind of mischief, has great experience, and knows just where he can attack every individual. We dare not think that he is far away from us, somewhere in India,

---

38   A Greek term meaning literally "rulers of this world," a designation for spirits or spiritual forces that exercise control over certain parts of the world or aspects of human life.

39   In the root Latin sense of "a learned person," that is, an expert.

/ neben vns / hinder vns / fu[e]r vns / vber vns / Ja er ist bey vns in
der kamer / bette / tische / wo wir gehen / stehen / sitzen oder ligen
/ Das vns wol not ist / Gott vmb hu[e]lffe zu bitten.

Wo vermanet vns die Schrifft / zur verleuckung der Welt?
Also sagt Johannes in seiner [E3v] ersten Epistel am 2. Capitel /
Habt nicht lieb die Welt / noch was in der Welt ist / So jemand die
Welt lieb hat / in dem ist nicht die liebe des Vaters / Denn alles was
in der Welt ist (Nemlich des fleisches lust / vnd der augen lust / vnd
hoffertiges leben) ist nicht vom Vater / sondern von der Welt / vnd
die Welt vergehet mit jrer lust. Vnd Sanct Jacob am 4. Wer der Welt
Freund sein wil / der wird Gottes Feind.

Was ist die Welt fur ein ding?
Die Welt ist des Teuffels Reich Paradis vnd Lusthaus / So ist der
Teuffel / Gottes vnd aller Christen abgesagter Feind / thut jnen das
ergest vnd leidest. Was nu in der Welt ist / das ist auch Gottes vnd aller
Christen Feind / Jnn der Welt aber / ist Weisheit / Gewalt / eusserliche
Heiligkeit vnd Gleisnerey / [E4r] Falsche lere / verfu[e]rung / Ketzerey
/ Jrthumb / Rotten vnd Secten / die toben alle widder Christum.
Christus gibt der Welt den Tittel / nennet sie eine Mordgruben / vnd
ein Lu[e]genhaus / Den Schilt hengt er der Welt vber die Thu[e]r /
Joha. 8. Dieweil wir hie auff Erden sind / mu[e]ssen wir vns des erwe-
gen / das wir in solcher Herberge sind / da der Wirt ein Schalck / ein
Mo[e]rder / vnd ein Lu[e]gener ist. Denn jnn diesem Gasthoffe des
Teuffels / gehets nicht anders zu / Morden vnd liegen / das ist sein
Handel vnd Haushalten / Wer seines Hoffgesinds ist / der mus jm
darzu helffen / Wer sein Gast ist / der mus solchs erwarten. Darumb
spricht Ciprianus / Wir stehen hie teglich vnter den waffen des Teuffels
/ die vnter vns hawen vnd stechen / wie in einen [E4v] Wald / da man
die axt sihet blitzen / vnd wollen stets die Christen zu bodem hawen.

Africa, or in the land of the Moors,[40] but he is right with us, next to us, behind us, in front of us, over us. Yes, he is with us in our rooms, in bed, at the table, wherever we walk, stand, sit, or lie down. Therefore, it is necessary for us to ask God for help.

Where does Scripture admonish us to deny the world?

John says in his first epistle, chapter two [:15], "do not love the world, or the things in the world. The love of the Father is not in the person who loves the world. For all that is in the world (namely the desire of the flesh and the desire of the eye and pride in riches) is not of the Father but of the world, and the world is passing away with its desires." And Saint James in his fourth chapter [:4]: "Whoever wants to be the world's friend is God's enemy."

What sort of thing is the world?

The world is the devil's realm, paradise, and hideaway.[41] As the devil is the avowed enemy of God and all Christians, he treats them in the worst and most harmful way possible. What then is in the world is also the enemy of God and all Christians. In the world there is wisdom, power, outward holiness and hypocrisy, false teaching, seduction, heresy, error, factions and sects, which all rage against Christ. Christ gives the world the label "open grave and a house of lies." He hangs that sign over its door, John 8 [:44][42] As long as we are in the world, we must remind ourselves that we are in an inn in which the proprietor is a scoundrel, a murderer, and a liar. For in this hotel of the devil, there is nothing else but murder and lying. That is the way he conducts his business, the way he runs his establishment. Whoever is his employee must help him to do this. Whoever is his guest must expect this sort of thing. Therefore Cyprian said, "We stand here daily under the devil's weapons, which chop and swing at us, as in a forest where you see the flash of the ax. He is always trying to chop the Christians to the ground."[43] The dan-

---

40   A designation used in the sixteenth century both for Ethiopia and for western sub-Saharan Africa.

41   The German "Lusthaus" refers to a summer home or castle.

42   Spangenberg attributes to the world the characteristics Christ assigns to the devil in John 8:44.

43   Cyprian (200-258), bishop of Carthage in north Africa, was widely-read in the Middle Ages. The precise citation which Spangenberg used cannot

Die geferligkeiten sind gros vnd mancherley / Der Weg ist schlipfrich / Die Feinde sind listig vnd mechtig / So sind wir Schwach / vnd tragen vnsern Schatz in jrdischen gefessen 2. Corinth. 4. Vnd stehen in grosser fahr vnd angst / auff allen seiten. Zur rechten / fechten vns an Rotten vnd Secten. Zur lincken / der Tu[e]rck / mit Morden vnd wu[e]rgen. Forne / die Papisten vnd Werckheiligen. Hinden / Ju[e]den vnd Heiden / Tyrannen / etc. Oben vnd vnten / alle Hellische Geister / Vnd im Summa / wo wir vns hin keren / so sehen wir nichts gutes / Nur bo[e]se Exempel / Ergernisse / hoffart / geitz / vnzucht / hass / etc. Wir ho[e]ren nichzs guts / Nur vnnu[e]tze wort / falsche Lere / Liegen / [E5r] triegen / fluchen / schweren etc. Zu Hofe findet man bo[e]se Radgeber / Heuchler / Finatzer. Jnn Stedten / zwispalt / vneinigkeit vnd falscheit. Jnn Hendel / betrug etc. Jnn Do[e]rffern / vngehorsam / list vnd betrigligkeit. Bey den Geistlichen / findet man die Grundsuppe aller vntugent / Hurerey / wucher / Gottslesterung / heucheley / falsche Heiligkeit / Das vns abermal wol not ist / Gott vmb hu[e]lffe vnd beistand zu bitten.

Wo vermanet vns die Schrifft zur verleuckung des eigen fleisches?
Also sagt Christus Luc. 14. So jemand zu mir ko[e]mpt / vnd hasset nicht sein vater vnd mutter / weib / kind bruder / schwester / Auch dazu sein eigen Leben / der kan nicht mein Ju[e]nger sein. Vnd Sanct Paulus Gala. 5. Welche Chri- [E5v] stum angeho[e]ren / die Creuzigen jr fleisch / sampt den lu[e]sten vnd begirden.

Was ist Fleisch fur ein ding?
Fleisch vnd blut heisset in der Schrifft / ein Adams kind / das ist / einen Menschen / der vol su[e]nd ist / in su[e]nden empfangen / in su[e]nden geborn / vnd in su[e]nden lebt / Jst vol hoffart / geitz / vnzucht / hass / vnd neid / Jst ein lu[e]gener / liebt sich selbs / kan keine strafe leiden / handelt jmerdar widder Gott / vnd ist doch staub vnd aschen / ja ein speise der wu[e]rmer. Beume vnd Kreuter bringen scho[e]ne blumen / bletter / vnd liebliche fru[e]chte / Der Mensche bringt nur vnzifer vnd vnflat. Vnd ist keiner nie so Lieb gewest / wenn er tod ist / man tregt jn zum grabe / vnd scharret zu. Noch darff ein solche arme Creatur / ein [E6r] elende Wasserblasen / vnd madensack / widder Gott seinen Schepffer vnd Heiland / sich aufflehnen. Aber Gott ist droben / der wehret den Beumen / das sie nicht bis in Himel

gers are large and varied. The way is slippery. The enemies are tricky and powerful. We are weak and carry our treasure in earthen vessels, 2 Corinthians 4 [:7]. We stand in the midst of great danger and terror on all sides. On the right factions and sects attack us. On the left the Turk is there with murder and slaughter. Ahead of us are papists and the works-righteous. Behind us are Jews and pagans, tyrants, etc. Above us and below us are all the hellish spirits. In summary, wherever we turn, we see nothing good, only evil examples, offenses, arrogance, greed, fornication, hatred, etc. We hear nothing good, only unprofitable words, false teaching, lies, deceit, curses, swearing, etc. At [princely] courts there are evil counselors, hypocrites, financial manipulators. In the towns there is division, disunity, and bad faith. In commerce there is dishonesty, etc., in the villages disobedience, deception, and cheating. Among the clergy the dregs of all vices are to be found: whoring, usury, blasphemy, hypocrisy, false holiness. Again, it is really necessary to pray to God for help and support.

Where does Scripture admonish us to deny our own flesh?
Christ says in Luke 14 [:26], "Whoever comes to me and does not hate father and mother, wife and children, brothers and sisters, even his own life, cannot be my disciple." And Saint Paul says in Galatians 5 [:24], "Those who belong to Christ crucify their flesh, with its passions and desires."

What sort of thing is the flesh?
Flesh and blood refers to a child of Adam in the Scripture, that is, a human being who is full of sin, conceived in sin, born in sin, who lives in sin and is full of arrogance, greed, fornication, hate, and envy, a liar, who loves himself and cannot take rebuke. He is always acting against God and is just dust and ashes, indeed, food for worms. Trees and plants produce beautiful flowers, leaves, and delightful fruit. The human being produces only vermin and garbage. A person is never so well regarded as when he is dead, carried to the grave, and lies under the dirt. Nonetheless, such a poor creature, a miserable water blister and bag of maggots, finds rest in God, his creator and savior. But God is above. He puts limits on the trees so that they do not grow up to heaven.

---

be found in Cyprian's works. It is possible that he was citing inexactly from memory or from a false attribution in a medieval collection of citations of the Fathers.

wachssen. Was sich vermisset in seinem eigen Namen vber Gott zu steigen / das stu[e]rtzet er widder herunter in des Teuffels Namen. Also bleiben nu diese Sprichwo[e]rter war / Homo homini lupus / Ein Mensch ist des andern Wolff. ja Teuffel. Jtem / Einen jglichen Menschen sollen wir halten / wie einen heiligen Engel / Aber sich fur jm hu[e]ten / wie fur dem leidigen Teuffel / Es sey denn / das er new geboren sey in Christo / Da heisset es / Homo homini Deus.

Wo vermanet vns die Schrifft / zu der vbung des Glaubens?
Also sagt Christus / Luce 13. [E6v] Ringet darnach / das jhr durch die enge Pforte eingehet / Denn viel werden darnach trachten / wie sie hinein komen / vnd werdens nicht thun ko[e]nnen. Vnd Johan. 6. da jn die die Ju[e]den fragten / Was sollen wir thun / das wir Gottes werck wircken? Antwortet Christus / Das ist Gottes werck / das jr an Den gleubt / den Er gesand hat.

Was ist der Glaube?
Der Glaube ist ein starcke zuuersicht / vnd ein gewisse hoffnung der ding / die man nicht fur augen sihet Hebre. 11. Aber furnemlich / ist der Glaube nichts anders / denn ein gewisse zuuersicht vnd vertrawen auff die barmhertzigkeit Gottes / welche vns zugesagt ist / vmb seines Sons Christi willen.

Was wirckt solcher Glaube?
Ein solcher Glaube wirckt viel gutes.

[E7r] 1 Eine sonderliche liebe zu Christo / Das ich Christum allein gros achte / Liebe / Ehre vnd Preis / als Den mir der Vater zum Mitler / Heiland vnd Seligmacher / gegeben hat / Der mir allein gnugsam ist / in all meinem anligen zu helffen / Jnn Dem all mein trost ist / Den ich sonst in keiner Creatur finden mag.

2 Eine innbru[e]nstige liebe gegem [!] dem Nehisten / Also / das der mensch seinem Nehisten thut / wie jm Christus gethan hat / Dienet jederman mit freuden.

3 Ein trotzig hertz / das weder Teuffel / noch Tyrannen fu[e]rchtet / leidet vnd duldet / was zu leiden ist / Ja wagets auff Gott / Es sey jnn anfechtung / verfolgung / im leben oder im tod / so lesset ers Gott walten.

Whatever endeavors to rise above God in its own name plunges down in the name of the devil. This proverb remains true: *Homo homini lupus*, one person acts like a wolf toward others. Indeed, a devil. We should regard every human being as a holy angel but guard ourselves against him as we would against the accursed devil, unless he is newborn in Christ. That means *Homo homini Deus* ["a person treats other people as God treats them"].

Where does Scripture admonish us to practice the faith?
Christ says in Luke 13 [:24], "Strive to enter through the narrow gate. For many try to enter and will not be able to do that." John 6 [:29], when the Jews asked, "What shall we do to carry out the work of God?" Christ answered, "This is God's work, that you believe on him whom he has sent."

What is faith?
Faith is a strong confidence and a certain hope for things which cannot be seen with the eyes, Hebrews 11 [:1]. But above all, faith is nothing else than a certain hope and trust in God's mercy, which is promised to us for the sake of Christ, his Son.

What does this kind of faith produce?
This kind of faith produces many good things.

1 a special love for Christ, so that I regard Christ alone as great and give him love, honor and praise, as the one whom the Father has given me as mediator, deliverer, and savior, who alone is sufficient to help me in all my concerns. In him rests my entire comfort, which I find apart from him in nothing he has created.

2 a fervent love for my neighbor, that is, that a person acts toward his neighbor as Christ has acted toward him, serving everyone with joy.

3 a defiant heart that fears neither the devil nor tyrants and bears and puts up with whatever suffering comes. Indeed, such a heart puts all confidence in God. Whether it be in spiritual struggles, persecution, in life or in death, it lets God take care of things.

[E7v] 4 Ein fro[e]lich vnd friedsam Gewissen / vnd reiniget das hertz von allen Su[e]nden / Denn Christus ist allein das rechte Osterlamb / das der Welt su[e]nde tregt / Johan. 1.

5 Der Glaub macht allein from vnd gerecht / vnd errettet vom Teuffel / Tod / Su[e]nd vnd Helle / Von Gottes zorn vnd vngnade / Joha. 3. Wer an Christum gleubt / der wird nicht gerichtet / Wer aber nicht gleubt / der ist schon gerichtet.

Wo vermanet vns die Schrifft / zur Liebe?

Also sagt Christus Johan. 13. Ein new Gebot gebe ich euch / das jr euch vntereinander liebet / wie ich euch geliebet hab / Dabey wird jederman erkennen / das jhr meine Ju[e]nger seid / so jhr euch vntereinander liebet. Vnd Esaie am 58. [E8r] Capitel / Brich dem Hungerigen dein brod / Vnd die so im elend sind / fu[e]re in dein Haus. So du einen nacketen sihest / so kleide jhn / vnd entzeuch dich nicht von deinem Fleisch.

Was ist die Liebe?

Augustinus in einem Sermon beschreibt die Liebe also / Die Liebe ist ein heilsam band / der hertzen vnd gemu[e]te / mit welcher / der arm reich ist / vnd on welche der reich arm ist. Die Liebe ist im vnglu[e]ck gedu[e]ltig / im glu[e]ck messig / im leiden starck / jnn der anfechtung vnerschrocken / jnn Gastfrey willig / jnn allen guten Wercken fro[e]lich.

Was wirckt die Liebe?

Also spricht S. Paulus 1. Corin 13. Die Liebe ist langmu[e]tig vnd [E8v] freundlich / Die Liebe eiuert nicht / Die Liebe schalcket nicht / Sie blehet sich nicht / Sie stellet sich nicht vngeberdig / Sie suchet nicht das jre / Sie lesset sich nicht erbittern / Sie gedenckt nichts arges / Sie frewet sich nicht der vngerechtigkeit / Sie frewet sich aber der warheit / Sie vertregt alles / Sie gleubt alles / Sie hoffet alles / Sie duldet alles / Die Liebe wird nicht mu[e]de. Vnd Roma. 12. setzet er auch viel fru[e]chte der Liebe / vnd an andern o[e]rten mehr.

Wo vermanet vns die Schrifft / zur to[e]dtung des Fleisches / Vnd erneuerung des Geistes?

4 a happy and peaceful conscience that cleanses the heart of all sin. For Christ alone is the true paschal lamb, who bears the sins of the world, John 1 [:29].

5 This faith alone makes people upright and righteous and saves them from the devil, death, sin and hell, from God's wrath and disfavor, John 3 [:18]: "Whoever believes in Christ is not judged. Whoever does not believe has been judged already."

Where does Scripture admonish us to love?

Christ says, John 13 [:34], "A new command I give you, that you love one another as I have loved you. By this everyone will recognize that you are my disciples, that you love one another." And in Isaiah 58 [:7]: "Bring the hungry your bread and welcome those who are in misery into your house. When you see someone naked, give him clothes, and do not hide yourself from your own kin."

What is love?

Augustine describes love in a sermon in this way: "Love is a wholesome bonding of hearts and minds, with which the poor are rich and without which the rich are poor. Love is patient in misfortune, moderate in fortune, strong in suffering, unshakable in spiritual struggles, spontaneous in hospitality, and joyous in all good works."[44]

What does love produce?

Saint Paul says in 1 Corinthians 13 [:4-7]: "Love is patient and kind. Love is not envious. Love does not boast and is not arrogant. It is not rude. It does not insist on its own way. It is not irritable or resentful. It does not rejoice in wrongdoing but rejoices in the truth. It bears all things, it trusts all things, it hopes all things, it endures all things. Love does not become weary." And in Romans 12 [:9-21] he presents many fruits of love, and does so also in even more places.

Where does Scripture admonish us to the mortification of the flesh and the renewal of the spirit?

---

44 Augustine (354-430), bishop of Hippo, perhaps the most influential church father in medieval theology and a favorite of Evangelical reformers, including Luther and his Wittenberg colleagues. This appears to be a paraphrase of a passage in Augustine.

Also sagt S. Paulus zun Ephe. am 4. Capitel / Legt von euch ab /
nach dem vorigen wandel / den alten Menschen / der durch lu[e]ste
im jrthumb sich verterbet / Ernewert [F1r] euch aber im Geist ewres
gemu[e]tes / vnd zihet den newen Menschen an / der nach Gott geschaffen ist / jnn rechtschaffner gerechtigkeit vnd heiligkeit.

Und Colloss. 3. To[e]dtet ewere glieder / die auff Erden sind / Hurerey
/ vnreinigkeit / lu[e]ste / bo[e]se begirde / vnkeuscheit / vnd den geitz
/ welches ist Abgo[e]tterey.

Und Christus sagt / Luce 21. Hu[e]tet euch / das ewre hertzen nicht
beschwert werden mit fressen vnd sauffen / vnd mit sorge der narung /
vnd kome dieser Tag schnel vber euch. Vnd Gala. 5. sagt Paulus / Wandelt
im Geist / so werdet ir die lu[e]ste des fleisches nicht volnbringen.

Wenn hebt sich die to[e]dung des fleisches an?
Jnn der Tauff / wenn der Prie- [F1v] ster das kind mit wasser be-
geust odder einsenckt / im Namen des Vaters / vnd des Sons / vnd
des Heiligen Geistes

Wenn wird sie volnbracht?
Jm sterben / wenn das fleisch zu staub vnd asschen wird.

Wenn hebt sich die ernewerung des Geistes an?
Wenn der Priester das Kind aus der Tauff hebt.

Wenn wird sie volnbracht?
Am Ju[e]ngsten tage / wenn wir widder auffstehen / mit leib vnd
seele / Da werden wir recht aus der Tauffe gehaben / vnd mit dem
kleide der Vnschuld bekleidet / Von den lieben Engeln getragen jnns
ewige Leben / Matth. 13.

Mu[e]ssen alle Christliche Ritter / diese drey stu[e]ck haben?
Wir haben sie in der Tauff ge- [F2r] lobt / vnd zu halten zugesagt
/ nemlich / dem Teuffel vnd all seinem wesen zu entsagen / Jnn Gott
Vater / Son / vnd den heiligen Geist / gleuben / vnd solchen Glauben
auch mit der that gegen dem Nehisten bezeugen / Den alten Adam /
das su[e]ndliche fleisch to[e]dten / Die bo[e]sen lu[e]ste dempffen /
vnd ein new Creatur Gottes werden / Darauff sind wir getaufft / vnd
jnn Gottes Register geschrieben / vnd ist vns der Sold / das ewige
Leben / zugesagt.

Paul says in Ephesians 4 [:22-25], "Lay aside your former way of life, the old creature, corrupted and deluded by its lusts, and put on the new creature, created according to the likeness of God, in true righteousness and holiness."

In Colossians 3 [:5]: "Put to death whatever in you that is earthly, fornication, impurity, passion, evil desire, unchastity, and greed, which is idolatry."

In Luke 21 [:34], Christ says, "Be on guard so that your hearts are not weighed down with dissipation and drunkenness and worries about nourishment [with the result that] that day catch you unexpectedly." And in Galatians 5 [:16] Paul says, "Live in the Spirit, and you will not gratify the desires of the flesh."

When does the mortification of the flesh begin?
In baptism, when the priest pours water over the child or immerses it, in the name of the Father and of the Son and of the Holy Spirit.

When is it completed?
In death when the flesh becomes dust and ashes.

When does the renewal of the spirit begin?
When the priest lifts the child out of the water [of baptism].

When is it completed?
On the Last Day, when we rise again in body and soul. Then we will be truly lifted up out of our baptism, and we will be clothed with the garment of innocence and carried into eternal life by the dear angels, Matthew 13 [perhaps a paraphrase of verses 41-43].

Must all Christian knights have these three elements?
We have pledged [to do] them in baptism and promised to practice them, namely to renounce the devil and all his ways; to believe in God, Father, Son, and Holy Spirit; and to give witness to this faith with our actions toward our neighbor, to mortify the Old Adam, that is, the sinful flesh, to suppress evil desires, and to become God's new creature. To that end we have been baptized and written into God's record book. The reward of eternal life has been promised to us.

Mit wie viel Feinden mus ein Christlicher Ritter kempffen?
Mit dreien Heubtfeinden (wie gesagt ist) Mit dem Teuffel / Welt
vnd eigenem Fleisch / die jhm nimmermehr kein ruge lassen / Auch
keinen vertracht leiden / noch friede annemen.

[F2v] Wie thut er im denn / das er sich dieser Feinde erwehre?
Sanct Paulus zeigt allen Christen einen Harnisch / Wehre vnd Waffen
/ damit sie sich fur solchen grewlichen Feinden mo[e]gen entsetzen /
Ephe. 6. vnd sagt also. Meine Bru[e]der / seid starck jnn dem HErrn
/ vnd jnn der Macht seiner stercke / zihet an den Harnisch Gottes /
das jr bestehen ku[e]nd / gegen den listigen anlauff des Teuffels. Vnd
weiter sagt er /
So stehet nu vmbgu[e]rtet ewre Lenden mit warheit / Vnd angezogen mit dem Krebs der Gerechtigkeit / vnd gestieffelt an fu[e]ssen
mit dem Euangelio des friedes / damit jr bereit seid / Fur allen dingen
aber / ergreifft den Schild des Glaubens / mit welchem jhr ausleschen
ku[e]nd / alle fewrige Pfeile des Bo[e]se- [F3r] wichts / Vnd nemet
den Helm des Heils / Vnd das schwerd des Geistes / welches ist das
Wort Gottes.
Da gibt vns Sanct Paulus / aus seiner Harnisch Kamer / den rechten
Harnisch / Nemlich / Ein Gu[e]rtel / Schuch oder Stiefel / ein Pantzer
oder Krebs / ein Schild / ein Helm / vnd ein Schwerd.

Was ist der Gu[e]rtel der Warheit?
Nichts anders / denn das wir ein rechtschaffen leben fu[e]ren / das
kein heucheley / sondern ernst sey / Das wir vns des Worts vnd des
Glaubens / mit ernst annemen / Denn wer in der Christenheit sein wil
/ vnd sich der sache nicht mit ernst annimpt / sondern lesset sich nur
vnter den hauffen mit zelen / wil mit geniessen / vnd doch nicht [F3v]
mit kempffen / der wird bald dem Teuffel zu teil werden / Denn er ist
nicht gegu[e]rtet / das ist / auffgeschu[e]rtzet / vnd geru[e]stet mit
Warheit / vnd rechtem ernst / als ein Kriegsman sein sol.

Against how many enemies must a Christian knight fight?

Against three chief enemies (as is said), against the devil, the world, and his own flesh, which never let him rest or enjoy a reprieve or find peace.

What can the knight do to defend himself against these enemies?

Saint Paul shows all Christians the armor, protective hardware, and weaponry, with which they may oppose these terrible enemies, and says in Ephesians 6 [:10-11, 14-17], "My brothers, be strong in the Lord and in the strength of his power. Put on the armor of God, so that you may be able to stand against the wiles of the devil." Further he says, "Stand, therefore, and fasten the belt of truth around your waist, and put on the breastplate of righteousness. As shoes for your feet put on the gospel of peace so that you may be prepared. Above all, take the shield of faith, with which you will be able to quench all the fiery arrows of the Evil One. Take the helmet of salvation and the sword of the Spirit, which is the Word of God."

There Paul gives us from his armor cabinet the real armor, namely a belt, shoes or boots, chain mail or breastplate, a shield, a helmet, and a sword.[45]

What is the belt of truth?

Nothing else than that we live an upright life, that is, without hypocrisy but rather with sobriety, that we take the Word and faith seriously. For some want to be a part of the Christian church[46] but do not take the matter seriously. They just want to be counted with the group and share the benefits but certainly not the battle. Such people will quickly take the side of the devil, for they are not girded, that is, not dressed and outfitted, with the truth and the kind of earnestness that is befitting for a warrior.

---

45   In the following presentation of the armor that Paul describes in Ephesians 6:13-17 Spangenberg used the description of each piece of the armor that Luther had put forth in his 1531 sermon on the passage, published in 1533: *Das Sechste Capitel der Epistel Pauli an die Epheser / Von der Christen harnisch vnd woffen* … (Wittenberg: Georg Rhau, 1533), WA 34,2: 399.3-406.2, sometimes citing longer or shorter passages from Luther directly, sometimes paraphrasing or summarizing his sermon.

46   The German "Christenheit," literally "Christendom" referred in Wittenberg usage specifically to the church.

Was ist der Krebs der Gerechtigkeit?

Nichts anders / denn ein gut Gewissen / ein vnschu[e]ldig / gerecht leben / vnd eusserlich wesen / gegen allen Menschen / Das man also lebe / das man niemands schaden noch leid thu / Sondern sich vleissige / jederman zu dienen / vnd guts zu thun / Also / das niemand vnser Gewissen beschu[e]ldigen / noch der Teuffel selbs / verklagen noch auffru[e]cken ko[e]nne / das wir nicht recht gelebt haben.

Was sind die Schuch vnd Stiefel / des Euangelischen Friedes?

Nichts anders / denn das wir [F4r] gegen jederman fried haben / jederman guts thun / mit helffen / radten / fordern / durch das Euangelion / Das wir dadurch bereit vnd geschickt wandeln ko[e]nnen / vnd in der bo[e]sen Welt hindurch komen / vngehindert. Ob gleich die Welt vntereinander Rumohr vnd eitel vnfried / hadder vnd zanck anrichtet / vnd der Leute bosheit vns auch reitzet zu zorn / rache / vngedult / Wir mu[e]ssen also geschickt sein / das wir ko[e]nnen die Bo[e]sen leiden / dulden vnd tragen / Vnd also durch gedult hindurch brechen / als durch einen dornichten weg. Es heisset / Wiltu Christen sein / so schicke dich zur gedult / Denn das Creutz wird nicht lang ausbleiben.

Was ist der Schild des Glaubens?

Nichts anders / denn der Glau- [F4v] be / der sich helt an das Wort von Christo. Denn wenn der Teuffel der Bo[e]sewicht / vns wil jnns Gewissen reissen / vnd vnser leben zu nicht machen / vnd wir sein zu lose gegu[e]rtet / haben nicht recht gelebt / auch jederman nicht gethan / wie wir solten / Das wir jhm als denn ko[e]nnen diesen Schild furwerfffen / Nemlich / vnsern HERRN Jhesum Christum im glauben gefasst / vnd sagen / Wolan / bin ich ein Su[e]nder / so ist der Man / der fur mich gestorben ist / heilig vnd rein / an den halt ich mich / Mein leben vnd thun / bleibe wo es ko[e]nne / Auff Christum verlasse ich mich / als auff meinen Schild / der mich kan decken vnd schu[e]tzen / sampt alle meinem leben / Der ist mir gewis / vnd bestehet wider alle Macht vnd Pforten der Hellen.

[F5r] Was ist der Helm des Heils?

Nichts anders / denn die hoffnung / vnd warten eines andern lebens / das droben im Himel ist / Vmb welches willen wir an Christum gleuben / vnd alles leiden / On welchen wir nicht ku[e]ndten ertragen / alle

What is the breastplate of righteousness?

Nothing other than a good conscience, an innocent and upright life and outward conduct toward all people, that a person lives in a way that does not harm nor hurt anyone, but is eager to serve everyone and do good to them. That means that no one can lay guilt on our conscience, nor can the devil himself accuse us or hold up to us that we have not lived an upright life.

What are the shoes or the boots of the peace of the gospel?

Nothing else than that we live in peace with everyone, do good to everyone, help them, give them good counsel, promote their interests through the gospel, so that on this basis we can live prepared and adroit and make our way through this evil world without hindrance. Although the world is stirring up dissatisfaction and discontent, strife and contention in its own ranks, and though the wickedness of people provokes us, too, to anger, revenge, and impatience, we must be prepared to suffer, tolerate, and bear the evil, and with patience move ahead, as if we were on a thorny path. That means that if you wish to be a Christian, make up your mind to be patient. For the cross will not stay away for long.

What is the shield of faith?

Nothing else than the faith that clings to the word about Christ. For when the devil, the scoundrel, wants to beat up on our consciences and undo our lives, and we are only loosely girded (that is, we have not lived in an upright manner and not done to others what we should have), then we can hold up against him this shield, that our faith grasps our Lord Jesus Christ, and says, "Hey, look, I am a sinner, but the man who has died for me is holy and pure. I am clinging to him, whatever my life and actions may be. I am relying on Christ, as on my shield that can cover and protect me, together with all my life, and that withstands the powers and portals of hell."

What is the helmet of salvation?

Nothing else than the hope and expectation of another life that is above, in heaven. Because of it we believe on Christ and suffer all things. Without him we could not bear all the blows that are aimed at our heads

die streiche / die man vns nach dem Heubt schlegt / vnd zu vnserm
leib vnd leben zusetzet. Aber das ist vnser Trost / das wir gleuben an
Jhesum Christum / der ein HERR vber Welt / Teuffel / vnd alles ist
/ durch Welchen wir gewislich ein ander Leben zu warten haben / das
Er vns aus allem vnglu[e]ck erlo[e]sen wird / vnd vnter die fu[e]sse
legen / was vns jtzt drenget vnd dru[e]cket.

Was ist das Schwerd des Geistes?

Nichts anders / denn das Wort Gottes / das sollen wir on vnter-
[F5v] las treiben vnd vben / mit leren / predigen / ho[e]ren / vnd
nicht lassen in der scheiden stecken / vnd verrosten / Denn also kan
es keine krafft beweisen / noch dem Teuffel schaden thun / Sondern
wir mu[e]ssen das schwerd vom ledder ziehen / zu[e]cken vnd fassen /
vnd stets damit vmb sich schlahen / durch leren vnd predigen / das es
jmmer fein scharff bleibe / Denn wo nicht wackere Prediger vnd trewe
Erbeiter sind / da thut der Teuffel mo[e]rdlichen schaden / Bringt auff
die Cantzel / an stadt der Warheit / eitel lu[e]gen / Macht alles vol
Rotterey / damit er die Kirche zutrennet vnd verterbet / Wie denn im
Bapsthumb geschehen ist.

Gib ein Exempel der Christlichen Ritterschafft / aus der heiligen
Schrifft?

Es ist schier kein Exempel jnn [F6r] der schrifft / daraus man die
Christliche Ritterschafft / hu[e]bscher ko[e]nne erlernen / denn die
Historia des Ausganges der Kinder Jsrael aus Egypto / durch das
Rote Meer / durch die Wu[e]sten / vnd durch den Jordan jns Land
Canaan.

Wie so?

Wie es da ergangen ist den Kindern Jsrael / leiblich / also gehet es
den Christen geistlich.

Was bedeut Pharaoh / vnd Egypten Land?

Pharao bedeut den leidigen Teuffel. Egypten land / das menschlich
leben / vor der Tauff.

Was bedeut das Rote Meer? Die Wu[e]sten? Der Jordan? vnd das
gelobte Land?

and are delivered to our body and life. But this is our consolation, that we believe in Jesus Christ, who is Lord over the world, the devil, and everything. Through him we certainly have another life to expect. We believe that he will deliver us out of all misfortune and put all that now is pressuring and oppressing us under his feet.

What is the sword of the Spirit?
Nothing else than the Word of God, with which we should be engaged and which we should be practicing all the time, by teaching it, preaching it, hearing it. We should not let it remain in the sheath and get rusty. For in that case it cannot demonstrate its power nor do the devil any harm. But we must draw the sword from the sheath, take it in hand, and grasp it, and be striking blows all around us all the time with our teaching and preaching, so that the Word always remains honed to a fine edge. For where there are not bold preachers and faithful workers, there the devil does murderous harm and brings to the pulpit pure lies instead of the truth. He fills the world with sects so that he may divide and corrupt the church, as happened in the papacy.

Give an example of Christian knighthood from Holy Scripture.
There is simply no example in Scripture from which one can learn in a more vivid fashion what Christian knighthood is than the story of the exodus of the children of Israel from Egypt through the Red Sea, though the wilderness, and through the Jordan into the land of Canaan.[47]

How is that?
The spiritual experience of Christians is like the physical experience of the children of Israel [Ex. 13-40, Jos. 3].

What do Pharaoh and Egypt represent?
Pharaoh represents the accursed devil. Egypt represents human life before baptism.

What do the Red Sea, the wilderness, the Jordan, and the Promised Land represent?

---

47   Spangenberg uses as the basis of his allegory the accounts of the exodus of the children of Israel out of Egypt, their wandering in the desert, and their entry into the promised land of Canaan in the books of Exodus and Numbers and Joshua 1-4.

Das Rote Meer / bedeut die Tauffe.

Die Wu[e]ste / diese betru[e]bte Welt.

[F6v] Der Jordan / den zeitlichen Tod.

Das gelobte Land / das ewige Leben.

Wie nu die Kinder Jsrael haben mu[e]ssen vier rheise thun / Die erste aus Egypto / an das Rote Meer. Die ander / vom Roten Meer / bis in die Wu[e]sten / an den Berg Sinai. Die dritte / aus der Wu[e]sten an den Jordan. Die vierde / durch den Jordan jnns gelobte Land / an den Berg Sion. Also mu[e]ssen wir Christen auch vier rheise thun / Die erste / Aus der Erbsu[e]nde zur Tauff. Die ander / aus der Tauff jnn diese bo[e]se Welt. Die dritte / aus der Welt in den zeitlichen Tod. Die vierde / aus dem natu[e]rlichen Tod / jnns ewige Leben. Vnd / wie die kinder Jsrael / in alle jhren rheisen / alle- [F7r] zeit widderstand hetten / vnd mit den Feinden (den Heiden) kempffen musten / Also mu[e]ssen wir Christen auch stets kempffen / mit dem Teuffel / Welt / vnd eigenem fleisch weil wir hie auff Erden leben.

Wie gehet dieser kampff zu?

Also gehet er zu / Wenn wir aus der Gewalt des Hellischen Pharao erlo[e]set / aus Egypten / das ist / aus dem su[e]ndlichen leben gangen / im Wasser vnd dem Heiligen Geist getaufft / vnd vnser su[e]nde im Roten Meer / in der Heiligen Tauffe / erseufft sind / Vnd komen in die Wu[e]sten dieser Welt / da es krimmelt vnd wimmelt von bo[e]sen Thieren / da nichts anders / denn eitel su[e]nde / laster / vntugent / vnd ergernis sind / So sollen wir nicht erschrecken / auch nicht widder zu ru[e]- [F7v] cke sehen jnn Egypten / Auch nicht stille stehen / sondern jemerdar fortfaren / von einer tugent in die ander / wie die kinder Jsrael rheiseten / von einem Lager zum andern. Komen wir jnn Mararath / jnn die bitter wasser der Trubsal / so sollen wir die bitterkeit senfftigen / vnd durch betrachtung des Leidens Christi / lindern vnd su[e]sse machen. Auch im hunger vnd durst / vnsere Seel vnd Geist / mit dem rechten Himelbrot / mit dem Worte Gottes vnd wasser / aus dem Felsen Christo / speisen / trencken / settigen / vnd stercken.

Wir sollen auch das Gesetz / von Gott gegeben / in vnser hertz bilden / vnd darnach leben / Vns selbs Gott dem Allmechtigen zum Tabernakel / Tempel vnd Wonung / heiligen / vnser Leibe vnd [F8r] Seele / zum lebendigen opffer / opffern. Alle Heiden am wege / Als / Amalekiter / Amoriter / Midianiter / vnd der gleichen / das ist / alle bo[e]se

The Red Sea represents baptism.
The wilderness represents this miserable world.
The Jordan represents temporal death.
The Promised Land represents eternal life.
The children of Israel had to complete four journeys, first out of Egypt to the Red Sea, the second from the Red Sea into the wilderness and to Mount Sinai, the third out of the wilderness to the Jordan, the fourth through the Jordan into the promised land, to Mount Zion. In the same way we Christians must complete four journeys. The first is out of original sin to baptism. The second is from baptism into this evil world. The third is from this evil world into temporal death. The fourth is from natural death into eternal life. Just as the children of Israel encountered continual resistance on all their journeys, and had to fight with their foes (the heathen), so we Christians have to fight continually with the devil, the world, and our own flesh while we live here on earth.

How does this battle take place?
It takes place when we are delivered from the power of hellish Pharaoh, from Egypt, that is, when we move out of this sinful life, when we are baptized with water and the Holy Spirit, and our sins are drowned in the Red Sea, in holy baptism. Then we come into the wilderness of this world, teeming and swarming with wild animals, which are nothing else than manifest sins, vice, wickedness, and malice. We should not be fearful, nor should we look back to Egypt. We should not stand still but always move on further, from one virtue to another, as the children of Israel kept on the move from one camping site to another. When we come to Marah [Ex. 15:23], to the bitter water of tribulation, we should take the edge off the bitterness and make it mild and sweet by meditating on the suffering of Christ. In hunger and thirst we should give our soul and spirit food and drink with the true bread of heaven, with God's Word and water from the rock of Christ, and thus make them satisfied and strengthen them.

We should engrave the law given by God upon our hearts and live according to it and dedicate our body and soul to God the Almighty himself in holiness as a tabernacle, temple, and dwelling place. We should sacrifice body and soul to him as a living sacrifice. With God's help and aid we should strike down and trample under foot all the heathen along

gedancken / wort vnd wercke / mit Gottes hu[e]lffe vnd beystand / herniderschlahen / vnd vnter die fu[e]sse tretten. Den Landku[e]ndigen / Das ist / den heiligen Propheten / Aposteln / vnd Euangelisten / Predigern / gleuben / Vnd vns nach dem Gelobten Lande / nach dem ewigen Leben / hertzlich sehnen. Wenn nu das stu[e]ndlin ko[e]mpt / vnd Gott vns foddert / So sollen wir auch durch den Jordan gehen / Das ist / den Tod willig annemen / Das sollen die Priester / mit der Archen / im mittel des Jordans stehen / bis das der durchgang geschehen ist / Das ist / sie sollen vns sterbenden menschen / mit dem Wort Gottes / beistehen / [F8v] Der Zusage Gottes erinnern / Vergebung der Su[e]nden / vmb Christus willen verku[e]ndigen / vnd zur gedult vnd bestendigkeit des Glaubens vermanen. Die vntern Wasser / das ist / zeitliche sorge / sollen wir lassen fu[e]rfliessen / Vnd wo die o[e]bern Wasser / das ist / die grewlichen Bilde des Teuffels / des Tods vnd der Hellen / durch jhr hohes auffsteigen / vns erschrecken wollten / als wolten sie vns vberfallen / so sollen wir mit einem festen Glauben an Christum / flugs furu[e]ber gehen / on alle furcht vnd schrecken / Bis wir komen mit trucken Fu[e]ssen / mit rechter gelassenheit vnd demut / an den Vfer des Himelischen Vaterlandes / zum ewigen Leben.

Was sagstu aber von den Bergen? Sinai vnd Zion?
Es sind drey namhafftige Ber- [G1r] ge jnn der Schrifft / auff welchen Gott am meisten / seine wunder vnd wercke / geoffenbart hat.

Welchs ist der erste Berg?
Der Berg Sinai / auff welchem Gott Moisi das Gesetz gegeben hat / in zweien steinern Taffeln. Da sahe man nichts anders / denn blitz vnd vngewitter / feurigen rauch vnd dampff / man ho[e]ret nichts anders / denn Donner / vnd die grausamen stimme der Posaunen / Da war nichts anders denn eitel furcht vnd schrecken / das auch die Kinder Jsrael Moisen baten / Er wolte mit jnen reden / vnd nicht der HERR / Sie kundten die Stimme Gottes nicht ertragen.
Dis alles zeigt an / die art / natur vnd eigenschafft des Gesetzes / das es nur schreckt / vnd richtet zorn an / Rom. 4.

[G1v] Welchs ist der ander Berg?

our path, the Amalekites, Amorites, Midianites,[48] and the like, that is, all evil thoughts, words, and deeds. We should believe those who know the land, that is, the holy prophets, apostles, and evangelists and preachers, and we should long for the Promised Land, for eternal life. When the last hour comes and God summons us, we should also go through the Jordan, that is, willingly accept death. The priests should then stand with the ark in the middle of the Jordan [Josh. 3:14-17], until the crossing has been accomplished, that is, they should assist us dying people with the Word of God, remind us of God's promise, proclaim the forgiveness of sins for Christ's sake, and admonish us to patience and steadfastness of faith. The water from below, that is, temporal cares, we should let flow by; and when the water from above, that is the horrifying machinations of the devil, of death and hell, want to terrify us by rising to great heights, as if they wanted to overpower us, we should pass on over at once, with a firm faith in Christ, without any fear and terror, until we come with dry feet, with true tranquility and humility, to the shore of the heavenly fatherland, to eternal life.

What do you say about the mountains? about Sinai and Zion?
There are three renowned mountains in Scripture on which God revealed most of his wonders and works.

Which is the first mountain?
Mount Sinai, on which God gave Moses the law in two stone tables [Ex. 31:18]. There nothing could be seen but lightning and storm, fiery smoke and steam. There was nothing to be heard but thunder and the terrifying sound of the trumpets. There was nothing else but raw fear and terror, [so bad] that even the children of Israel asked Moses to talk to them and not let the Lord talk to them [Ex. 20:18-21]. They could not bear the voice of God.
This all shows the essence, nature, and characteristics of the law: it only terrifies and delivers wrath, Romans 4 [:15].

Which is the second mountain?

---

48   The Amalekites (Num. 14:45, Deut. 25:17-18, Judg. 3:13-6:3), the Amorites (Num. 21:21-35, Deut. 3:8, 4:46-50, Judg. 1:34-35), and the Midianites (Num. 31:1-12, Judg. 6-8) were among the enemies of Israel, tribes against whom the children of Israel battled on their way to the Promised Land and as they took possession of it.

Der Berg Zion / Auff welchem Christus anfenglich sein heiliges
Euangelion hat verku[e]ndiget / im Tempel zu Jerusalem / Daselbs
viel vnd grosse Wunderwerck geu[e]bt / Auch durch sein leiden vnd
sterben / das Menschliche Geschlecht erlo[e]set / Widerumb aufferstanden vom Tode / Auffgefaren gen Himel / vnd den Heiligen Geist
gesand / Vnd seine Aposteln abgefertiget / das Euangelion zu predigen
in aller Welt.

Welchs ist der dritte Berg?
Der Berg Thabor / Auff welchem CHristus offt gebetet / vnd sich
fur seinen Ju[e]ngern / Petro / Johanne vnd Jacobo / Moise vnd Helia / verkleret hat. Da sahe man nichts anders / denn eitel liecht vnd
klarheit / Ho[e]rete nichts an- [G2r] ders / denn ein fein freundlichs
gespreche / Da war nichts anders / denn eitel freude vnd wonne / das
auch / S. Petrus fur freuden heraus fuhr / vnd sagte / HErr / hie ist
gut sein / Wiltu / so wollen wir drey Hu[e]tten machen / Dir eine /
Moisi eine / vnd Helia eine.
Dis alles zeiget an / die art / natur vnd eigenschafft des Euangelions
/ das es nur tro[e]stet / vnd erfrewet die hertzen.

Mus ein Christ auch auf diese Berge komen?
Ein jglicher Christ / der da gedenckt selig zu werden / der mus auff
diese drey Berge komen / nicht leiblich / sondern geistlich.
Erstlich / auff den Berg Sinai / daselbs das Gesetz / vnd die Zehen
Gebot lernen / und nicht allein lernen / sonder auch darnach leben.
[G2v] Dieweil wir aber befinden / das wir die Zehen Gebot / aus
vnsern krefften / aus fleisch vnd blut / nicht ko[e]nnen volnbringen
/ Vnd Gott wil sie dennoch / kurtzumb / von vns volnbracht vnd
erfu[e]llet haben / so mu[e]ssen wir von not wegen erschrecken / vnd
fur Gottes Gericht erzittern / vnd vns fur arme / verdampte Su[e]nder
bekennen / Vnd wo wir hie am Berge Sinai / mit Moise verblieben /
so weren wir verloren.
Darumb mu[e]ssen wir weiter rheisen / bis auff den Berg Zion. Vnd
hie auff dieser Rheise / mus Moises sterben vnd begraben werden /
Das man auch sein grab nicht wisse / Das ist / Hie mus fallen alles

Mount Zion,[49] on which Christ first proclaimed his holy gospel in the temple in Jerusalem, and there performed many great miracles. Through his suffering and death, he redeemed the human race, and rose again from the dead, ascended into heaven, and sent the Holy Spirit. He sent forth his disciples to preach the gospel in the entire world.

Which is the third mountain?

Mount Tabor,[50] on which Christ often prayed and on which he was transfigured in the presence of his disciples, Peter, James, and John, and Moses and Elijah. There nothing else could be seen but sheer light and radiance, and nothing else could be heard but a fine, friendly conversation. There was nothing else but sheer joy and delight, so that Saint Peter bubbled over with joy and said, "Lord, it is good to be here! If you wish, we will make three tents here, one for you, one for Moses, one for Elijah" [Matt. 17:1-8].

This shows the essence, nature, and characteristics of the gospel, that it gives comforts and joy to the heart.

Does a Christian have to come to these three mountains?

Every Christian who is planning to be saved must come to these three mountains, not physically but spiritually.

First, to Mount Sinai, to learn the law and the Ten Commandments, and not just learn them but also live according to them.

But because we find we cannot fulfill the Ten Commandments by our own powers, by our own flesh and blood, and God wants them kept and fulfilled by us in spite of that, pure and simple, we must necessarily be terrified and tremble in the face of God's judgment and confess that we are poor, condemned sinners. If we were to remain on Mount Sinai with Moses, we would be lost.

Therefore, we must journey further, to Mount Zion. On this journey Moses must die and be buried, and in such a way that his grave[site] is not known [Deut. 34:6]. That means that here all reliance on your

49 Mount Zion was the temple mount in Jerusalem.

50 Mount Tabor was believed in the Middle Ages to be the mountain on which Christ was transfigured (since Origen) and also that on which he appeared to more than five hundred disciples after his resurrection (since Theodosius). In the fourth century Saint Helen, the mother of Emperor Constantine, built a church on this mountain dedicated to the three apostles present at Christ's Transfiguration.

vertrawen auff eigne fro[e]migkeit vnd gerechtigkeit / Auff menschliche
wercke vnd verdienste / vnd mu[e]ssen allein Christum im glau-[G3r]
ben ergreiffen / Sein heiliges Euangelion / so er zu Zion vnd Jerusalem
geprediget hat / ho[e]ren / vnd mit ernst auffnemen / vnd vnser leben
darnach richten / Vnd jnn Summa / vnserm Nehisten thun / wie vns
der frome getrewe Christus gethan hat / Wo das geschicht / so sol vns
das Gesetz nicht anklagen / die Su[e]nde nicht beissen / der Tod nicht
schrecken / Sondern sollen haben vergebung der su[e]nde / vnd die
Zusage des ewigen Lebens.

Auff diesen zweien Bergen / vertreiben wir dis zeitlich leben / fallen
jmerdar von einem auff den andern / Jtzund sind wir vnter dem Gesetz / jtzt vnter dem Euangelio. Es ko[e]mpt wol / das wir widder in
Egypten / in das su[e]ndlich Leben / geradten / Balde jaget vns das
Gesetz widder zuru[e]ck gen Jerusalem / [G3v] an den Berg Zion / Das
geiegte / vnd dieser kampff / weret so lange / bis das das stu[e]ndlin
ko[e]mpt / das wir von hinnen sollen / Da mu[e]ssen wir auch auff
den Berg Thabor.

Der Berg Thabor / ist ein runder Berg / des Landes Galilee / ligt
im flachen felde / Vnd bedeut das selige sterben der Christen / Zu
welchem niemands ko[e]mpt / Er habe denn einen runden gesunden
Glauben zu Gott / vnd ein auffrichtig erhaben hertz / zu Go[e]ttlichen
himlischen dingen / Vnd sey in Galilea an der Grentz / in einem bus-
fertigen Christlichem Leben.

Was nu hie auff dem Berge Thabor geschehen ist / das wird in einem
jeglichen sterbenden Menschen auch ergehen. Denn wiewol die lieben
Aposteln mit CHRJSto [G4r] auff dem Berge sind / vnd sehen seine
Go[e]ttliche Klarheit vnd Herrligkeit / Sehen darzu Moisen vnd Heliam
/ Gesetz / Propheten / vnd alles verkleret / fein freudig vnd lu[e]stig /
Jdoch / weil Gott der Vater sich horen [!] lesst vom Himel / mit einer
grossen herrlichen Stimme / DJS JST mein lieber Son / an welchem
ich wolgefallen habe / DEN solt jr ho[e]ren / So ist menschliche Natur
so schwach / das sie fur der hohen Maiestet Gottes / nicht bestehen
kann / mus erschrecken vnd zu bodem fallen.

Hie ist nu die kunst / So wir jnn der letzten stunde / nach dem
schrecken des Gesetzes / die augen widder auffthun / vns vmbsehen /
vnd niemands sehen / denn allein CHRJstum / des Vaters Son / Das
wir als denn / jnn vnserm [G4v] hertzen alles faren lassen / Moisen /
Heliam / Aposteln / Jnn Summa / alle heilige menschen / alle Creaturn

own piety and righteousness, on human works and merit, must vanish and Christ alone must be grasped in faith. His holy gospel, which he proclaimed on Zion and in Jerusalem, must be heard and accepted sincerely, and our lives must be governed according to it. In summary, we must act toward our neighbor as the upright and faithful Christ acted. Where that happens, the law no longer accuses us, sin does not gnaw at us, death does not terrify us, but we have the forgiveness of sins and the promise of eternal life.

On these two mountains we while away this temporal life. We are always falling from one onto the other. At one time we are under the law, at another under the gospel. It happens that we wander once again into Egypt, into the life of sin, and immediately the law chases us back to Jerusalem, to Mount Zion. The chase and the struggle go on the whole time until our hour [of death] comes, when we are supposed to depart [this life]. Then we must go to Mount Tabor.

Mount Tabor is a round mountain in the land of Galilee. It lies in a flat field and represents the blessed death of the Christian. No one attains such a death without having a round,[51] sound faith in God and an upright heart uplifted to divine, heavenly things. Such a person is in Galilee, on the border,[52] in a repentant, Christian life.

What happened on Mount Tabor will also come to pass for every dying human being. For the dear apostles are with Christ on the mountain and see his divine radiance and glory; they see Moses and Elijah, the prophets, and everything transfigured, splendrous, joyous, and fantastic. Nonetheless, because they also hear the resounding majestic voice of God the Father from heaven, "This is my beloved Son, in whom I am well pleased. Listen to him!" human nature is so weak that they cannot stand in the presence of the lofty majesty of God and must feel terror and fall to the ground [Matt. 17:1-8].

This is the skill [that we need to learn:] that in our last hour, after the terror of the law, we again open our eyes, look around us, and see no one but Christ alone, the Son of the Father. Then in our hearts we let go of everything, Moses, Elijah, the apostles, in summary, all holy

---

51   Spangenberg made a word play with "round" in its geometric sense, describing the mountain, and in its metaphorical sense, "complete."

52   As the northernmost province in the Promised Land, Galilee represents for Spangenberg the Christian's living on the border between faith and disbelief, between obedience and disobedience, within the rhythm of daily repentance.

/ Ja auch vnsere eigene werck vnd verdienst etc. Vnd ergreiffen den
einigen Mitler / vnsern Heiland vnd Seligmacher Jhesum Christum /
Der vnsern nichtigen leib auch verkleren wird / das er ehnlich werde
seinem verklerten Leibe / Wie zun Philppern am 3. Cap. stehet / Auff
das wir (so die zeit vnsers abscheidens vorhanden ist / vnd wir Ritterlich gekempfft / vnd vnsern lauff volendet / vnd glauben gehalten
haben) tu[e]chtig vnd geschickt werden / die Kron der Gerechtigkeit
zu empfahen / vnd mit jm einzugehen / jnn sein verkleret Reich / jnn
das ewige Leben / Amen.

[G5r] Von der Papisten Ritterschafft.

Worinne stehet der Papisten Ritterschafft?

DER Papisten Ritterschafft stehet in geweihetem Wasser / Saltz /
Palmen / Wu[e]rtz / Wachs / Stein / Holtz / Glocken vnd Schellen
/ Denn mit solchem dinge / wollen sie den Teuffel veriagen / Gottes
gnade / vnd vergebung der su[e]nde erlangen.

Womit beweisen vnd bezeugen sie solche Ritterschafft?

Zu bekrefftigung solcher Ritterschafft / fu[e]ren sie das trefflich
Exempel / so jnn dem Marial geschrieben stehet.

Welch ist solch Exempel?

Ein Mo[e]rder / hett sein leben lang nie guts gethan / Der kam on
gefehr auff ein zeit in die Kirchen / [G5v] vnd sahe / das die Leute
Pfennige opfferten / da trat er auch hinzu / vnd opffert einen Pfenning
vnd ein Liechtlin auff den Altar. Es begab sich / das derselbige mo[e]rder
hernach / in seiner vbelthat ergriffen / vnd an Galgen gehangen ward /
Da wolten die Teuffel seine Seele zur Hellen fu[e]ren / Aber ein guter
Engel kam / vnd widerstund jnen / Sie zogen fur Gottes Gericht / Die
Teuffel klagten jhn an / das er sein lebenlang nie gutes gethan hette /
Aber der gute Engel zoch herfur einen Creutzpfenning / vnd ein Wa-

people, all creatures, and even our own works and merits, etc., and we grasp the only mediator, our savior and redeemer Jesus Christ. He will transfigure our worthless body so that it will be similar to his transfigured body, as it says in Philippians 3 [a paraphrase of verses 10-14], so that when the time of our departure is at hand, and we have fought the good fight and finished the race and kept the faith, we may be prepared and equipped to receive the crown of righteousness and to enter with him into his glorious kingdom, into eternal life. Amen

On the Knighthood of the Papists.

In what does the knighthood of the Papists consist?
The knighthood of the Papists consists of consecrated water, salt, palm branches, spices, wax, stones, wood, bells and the ringing of bells.[53] With such things they want to chase away the devil and attain God's grace and the forgiveness of sins.

How do they prove and support this kind of knighthood?
To confirm this kind of knighthood they refer to the superb example found in the "Mariale."[54]

What is this example?
A murderer had never done anything good his entire life. He came by chance one time into a church and saw that the people were contributing their pennies. He joined in and contributed a penny and a little candle on the altar. It came to pass some time later that this very murderer was arrested during a crime and hanged on the gallows. The devils wanted to take his soul to hell, but a good angel came and opposed them. They took their case before the court of God. The devils accused him of having done nothing good his entire life. But the good angel presented a penny with a cross on it and a little wax candle that he had made as a contribution on the altar. What happened? The judge rendered his verdict. The murderer was to defend himself against the devil. The angel gave him advice: he should take the penny with the

53   Spangenberg lists a series of objects associated with what the Lutheran reformers regarded as superstitious practices common in medieval piety.

54   The "Mariale" is a designation for texts of various genre relating to the Virgin Mary and used for devotional purposes in the Middle Ages. In various forms these collections of meditations existed from the twelfth century on.

chskertzlin / so er auff den Altar geopffert hett. Was geschach? Der
Richter gab das Vrteil / Der Mo[e]rder solt sich der Teuffel wehren /
Da gab jhm der Engel den radt / Er solte den Creutzpfenning jnn die
lincke hand nehmen / fur ein Schild / vnd die Kertzen jnn die [G6r]
rechte hand / fur ein Schwerd / vnd solte eitel Creutzschlege thun /
Das that er / vnd veriaget also den Teuffel / vnd gewan.

Haben sie der Exempel noch mehr?

Dis Exempel ist fast jr bester grund / Wiewol solcher schendlicher
lu[e]gen Exempel / alle jre Bu[e]cher vnd Predigstu[e]le vol gewest /
vnd noch sind / Da war kein hohe Schule / kein Stifft / kein Kloster /
ja kein Babst / kein Cardinal / kein Bisschoff / kein Doctor / der ein
wo[e]rtlin wider solche lu[e]gen geredt / geschrieben / odder geprediget
hett / Waren eitel stumme Hunde / die nicht bellen kundten / Wie
der Prophet klagt / Da man leret vnd prediget / das ein Pfenning vnd
Kertzlin / vnser lieben Frawen geopffert / ko[e]ndte einen Schalck /
einen Reuber vnd Mo[e]rder / on CHRJsto / on Glauben / von der
Hellen erret-[G6v] ten / vnd alle Teuffel veriagen / Damit Gott ge-
lestert / Christus Blut geschendet / vnd das gantze Euangelium / vnd
christlicher Glaube / zu nichte wird / Waren alle Predigte ko[e]stlich
gut / kein Ketzerey / kein Newerung / Sondern waren eitel gu[e]ldene
Christen.

Nu man aber leret vnd prediget / das Jhesus Christus sey vnser
einiger Mitler / Fu[e]rspecher / Heiland vnd Seligmacher / Vnd der
Glaub / der durch die Liebe wircket / allein From / Gerecht / vnd Selig
mache / vnd das wir allein durch das Blut Jhesu Christi / vergebung
der su[e]nden haben / werden sie toll vnd to[e]richt / wu[e]ten vnd
toben on alle mas / Suchen ausflucht vnd menschliche glo[e]slin / wo
sie ko[e]nnen / Da mus CHRJstus selbs ein Ketzer sein / Das Euan-
[G7r] gelium / ein Newerung / Die lieben Psalmen / Brodreigen /
Paulus habe wider sich selbs geschrieben / vnd an vielen o[e]rten den
rechten Grund nicht troffen. Jnn Summa/ Bey den Euangelischen sein
eitel ku[e]pfferne vnd hu[e]ltzerne Christen. Deo gratias.

Vom Misbrauch des Creutzes / Spehr / Nagel / vnd Krone Christi.

cross on it in his left hand as a shield, and the candle in the right hand as a sword, and simply make the sign of the cross repeatedly. He did that, and he chased the devil away and won the victory.

Is there another example?

This example is about the best proof although all of their books and preaching have been filled with examples of such shameful lies. There was no university, no foundation, no monastery, indeed no pope, cardinal, bishop or doctor, who dared to speak, write, or preach the slightest word against such lies. They were no more than mute hounds, who could not bark, as the prophet complains [Isa. 56:10]. It was taught and preached that a penny [contributed] or a candle [bought] for our dear lady [the Virgin Mary] could save any rogue, a robber or a murderer, without Christ, without faith, from hell, and chase away all devils. The result was that God was blasphemed, Christ's blood was profaned, and because of this the whole gospel and Christian faith were rendered useless. All sermons were delightfully good. There was no heresy, no innovations. They [the clergy of his day who were committed to the Roman party] were just sterling Christians.

Now it is taught and preached that Jesus Christ is our only mediator, advocate, deliverer, and savior, and that faith, which does its work through love, is the only thing that makes people upright, righteous, and blessed, and that we have the forgiveness of sins only through the blood of Jesus Christ. This makes them [the papal party] mad and foolish. They rage and rave uncontrollably and try to find a pretext and some human justification, wherever they can. Christ himself must be a heretic, the gospel an innovation, the dear Psalms songs to beg by.[55] Paul is said to have contradicted himself and to have argued on a false basis in many passages. To summarize, [they teach that] among the Evangelicals are no more than copper and wooden[56] Christians. *Deo gratias!* [(they say] ["Thanks be to God."]

On the Abuse of the Cross, Spear, Nails and Crown [of Thorns] of Christ

---

55   A reference to monastic begging that took place while the friars sang the Psalms on the streets.

56   That is, counterfeit and worthless.

AUff dem Berge Caluarie / stunden drey Creutz / Das Creutz CHristi / vnd der zweien Mo[e]rder. Das Creutz CHristi hat man geteilt jnn alle Welt / Darauff sind grosse Thumbkirchen / Klausen / vnd Capellen gestifft. Man hats in Golt / Silber vnd Eddelgestein gefasset / Tragens empor / vnd singen / Crucem tuam Domine adoramus Alleluia. Lanceam tuam Domin- [G7v] e adoramus. Das ist ein grosser misbrauch / Vnd geben damit selbs an tag / wer sie sind / Als wolten sie sagen / Schawet her / wir sind Papisten / bo[e]se Christen / wir lassen Gott den Schepffer faren / vnd halten vns an die Creatur. Lassen Christum vnd sein Wort / vnd beten an sein Creutz / Spehr / Nagel / vnd Kron. Aber Gott hat sie auch redlich bezalet / das sie offt ein stu[e]ck von der Mo[e]rder Creutz / oder sonst spehn von Galgen / an stadt des heiligen Creutzes / getragen vnd geehret haben / Denn es nicht mu[e]glich ist / das es alles vom Creutz Christi sein solt / das man hin vnd her / fur Christus Creutz helt vnd ehret.

Vom Misbrauch des Heilthums.

ALso gieng es auch mit dem Heilthumb / das man offt an stat der Heiligen Gebeine / bo[e]ser Menschen [G8r] oder Schelmen beine getragen vnd geehret hat / Ja wenn alle Co[e]rper der Gebeine / so in den grossen Processionen / vmbher getragen sind worden / jnn jrer substantz / weren gegenwertig gewest / solt man gar viel wu[e]nderlicher Thier fur augen gesehen haben. Also sol sie Gott blenden vnd verstocken. Weil sie das rechte Heilthumb Christi / Gottes Wort / verachten / sollen sie dieweil / an stadt des rechten Heilthumbs / Schelms beine tragen vnd ehren. Sie haben nicht allein das Creutz / Spehr / Nagel / Kron / sondern auch die Todtenbeine / zum Jnstrument vnd Werckzeug / jres Geitzes vnd Schinderey / gemacht.

Vom Misbrauch der Messe.

ALSO haben sie auch die Messe zum schendlichen Jarmarckt ge- [G8v] macht / vnd zum Opffer fur die lebendigen vnd todten / Vnd du[e]rffen sagen / Sie helffe Ex opere operato, sine bono motu vtentis.

On the Mount of Calvary stood three crosses, the cross of Christ and those of the two murderers [Matt. 27:32-38]. The cross of Christ was divided up [and distributed] into the entire world.[57] Huge churches manned by canons, isolated monasteries, and chapels were founded upon the basis of [a piece of the cross]. These pieces were set in gold, silver, and jewels, they were paraded around, and [those in the procession] sang, "We adore your cross, Lord. Alleluia. We adore your spear, Lord, Allelujah."[58] That is a great abuse. They disclose with this practice who they are. It is as if they say, "Look here! We are the Papists, bad Christians. We let God the Creator vanish, and we cling to what he has created. Leave Christ and his word alone. Pray to his cross, spear, nails, and crown." But God has also paid them a just wage in that often they are parading and honoring a piece of the murderer's cross, or some other chip of some gallows instead of the holy cross. For it is not possible that everything that is carried around, regarded, and honored as Christ's cross is really from Christ's cross.

On the Abuse of Relics
So it was also with relics. Often in place of the bones of the saints the bones of evil people or rogues were put on parade and honored. Indeed, if all the pieces of such bones which had been put on parade were assembled into what they really had been, it is said that many strange-looking animals would appear before their eyes.[59] In this manner God is said to have blinded them and hardened their hearts. In the meantime, because they despise the true holy object of Christ, God's Word, they are compelled to put the bones of rogues on parade and honor them. They have not only made the cross, spear, nails, crown, but also the bones of the dead an instrument and implement of their greed and swindling.

On the Abuse of the Mass
They have also made the Mass into a shameful carnival and into a sacrifice for the living and the dead. They dare to say that it provides

---

57　A reference to the sale of wood alleged to be parts of the cross of Christ as relics.

58　From a variation of the traditional Good Friday liturgy.

59　Spangenberg is repeating the charge that many relics presented to the faithful in medieval churches were in fact animal bones.

Was ku[e]ndte vnchristlichers gesagt werden / Sie geben fur / Missa / kome her von MisBrach / das ein Altar heisst / Daraus folge / das die Messe mu[e]sse ein Opffer sein / denn man pflege auff dem Altar zu opffern. Das ist ein jrthumb / Denn Missa ist ein Ju[e]disch wort / ko[e]mpt von Mas / heisset ein zusamen getragen Almos / Spende / oder steur / vmb der Priester vnd armen willen / Wie auch im anfang der Kirchen / solcher gebrauch geblieben ist / wie S. Paulus 1. Corin. 11. meldet / vnd anderswo mehr / Vnd heisset es Collecta odder Communio.

Also sagen sie auch / Das wort (Liturgia) heisse ein Opffer / [H1r] Das ist auch falsch / Liturgia / heisset ein gemein Dienstampt / als / da ein Priester die Leute absoluirt / Communiciret / Vnterricht / Leret vnd prediget.

Vom Misbrauch der heiligen Schrift

Also gauckeln sie auch im Testament Christi / Sagen / Hoc facite, heisse / Opffert. Vnd der jrrigen stu[e]cke haben sie viel.

Aus dem Spruch des 51. Psalmen / Besprenge mich mit Jsopen / haben sie das sprengen mit geweihetem wasser erticht.

help "*Ex opere operato, sine bono motu vtentis.*"[60] What more unchristian could be said! They claim that "Missa" comes from "MisBrach," which means "altar." They deduce from that that the Mass must be a sacrifice, for sacrifices are made on the altar. This is an error, for "Missa" is a Jewish word, comes from "Mas," and means a collection of alms, gifts, or levy for the sake of the priests or the poor.[61] This custom remained in the first years of the church's existence, as Saint Paul reports in 1 Corinthians 11 [perhaps a reference to the support gathered for Paul mentioned in 2 Corinthians 11:8] and in other passages. It means a collection or a sharing.

They also say that the word "Liturgia" means a sacrifice. That is false. "Liturgia" means a general office of service, as when a priest absolves, communes, instructs, teaches and preaches to the people.[62]

On the Abuse of Holy Scripture

Thus, they play around with the testament of Christ and say that "This do" means "Sacrifice" [Luke 22:19]. They have many passages with similar errors.

From the passage in Psalm 51 [:7], "Sprinkle me with hyssop," they have invented sprinkling with holy water.[63]

---

60   Literally, "accomplished by the act of doing [the ritual], without need of proper motivation [understood by the Lutherans as faith in Christ]."

61   Scholars today are agreed that both this medieval interpretation of the word and also Spangenberg's are false. The term comes from the Latin "Ite, *missa est*," the formula for dismissing the people at the end of the worship service.

62   "Liturgia" originally did mean "public service," from the personal noun for one who executed such an office, and then the word came to designate in ancient Greek religion a worship service.

63   The custom of providing consecrated or "holy" water in the church goes back to the fourth century. This water was believed to have magical powers by the vast majority of the population and was used to ward off evil of various sorts.

Aus dem Spruch des 119. Psalmen / Jch lobe dich des tages sieben mal / berewen sie die sieben tagezeit / so sie Horas Cononicas [!] nennen.

[H1v] Aus dem Spruch / 2. Machabeo.12. Die Seelmesse.

Aus dem Spruch des 66. Psalmen / Wir sind in Fewer vnd Wasser komen / Das Fegefewer.

Aus dem Spruch Apoca. 14. Jre wercke folgen jnen nach / Beweren sie Vigilig vnd Seelmessen / Psalter lesen / den Dreissigsten / Jar

From the passage in Psalm 119 [:164], "I will praise you seven times a day," they prove[64] the seven times of the day that they call the "Horas canonicas."[65]

From the passage in 2 Maccaebees 12 [:39-46] [they prove] the mass for [dead] souls.[66]

From the passage in Psalm 66 [:12], "We have come in fire and water," [they prove] purgatory.[67]

From the passage in Revelation 14 [:13], "Your works follow you" they prove vigils and masses for [dead] souls,[68] reading of the psalter,[69] the Thirtieth,[70] annual remembrances,[71] pilgrimages,[72] the priests'

---

64   read "beweren" instead of "berewen."

65   "Horas canonicas," the "canonical hours," refers to the program of formal devotions which monks and nuns in every monastery held seven times a day.

66   Masses celebrated for the dead were believed to relieve the suffering of Christians in purgatory.

67   Purgatory is in Roman Catholic theology the place or condition in which Christians receive the punishments due the temporal consequences of their sins after death. Popular belief ignored the distinction between the actual forgiveness of the eternal consequences of sin in the sacrament of penance and this punishment for the temporal consequences in purgatory, and the widespread opinion that suffering in purgatory earned God's favor was sharply rejected by the reformers.

68   Vigils were devotional exercises, particularly those conducted on the eve of a festival or holy day, through which merit in God's sight was won according to medieval teaching.

69   Reading of the psalter had, in the view of many Evangelical reformers, become a mechanical work defined as meritorious by the monastic orders.

70   A designation for several pious practices that involved the repetition of the rosary, other prayers, a mass, etc., thirty times to attain benefits for oneself or relatives and friends who had died and gone to purgatory.

71   A designation for masses said in behalf of the deceased on the anniversary of their death.

72   Pilgrimages were journeys made to holy shrines, chiefly for the purposes of venerating relics, through which Christians could win favor from God and merit for salvation.

gedechtnis / Walfarten / der Pfaffen Caland / Bruderschafft / vnd
ander lappenwerck.

Also ist das auch ein grobe verstockte blindheit / das sie du[e]rffen
sagen / schreiben vnd predigen / der Bapst vnd die Prelaten der
Ro[e]mischen Kirchen / mo[e]gen das Euangelium vnd Christus wort
vnd ordnung / nach jrem gefallen / endern / So doch alle Engel / ja
auch Hei-[H2r] ligen / in Himel vnd Erden / nicht macht haben / ein
tu[e]ttel oder buchstaben zu endern.

Jch wil setzen / wenn der jtzige Bapst vnd Prelaten gewalt hetten
/ das Euangelium vnd Gottes wort zu endern / So mo[e]chten vber
vierzig oder funffzig Jar andere komen / vnd auch also thun / Was wolt
aber zu letzt draus werden? Were doch in dem fall / der Handwercker
/ Schuster vnd Schneider lere / statut vnd ordnung / gewisser vnd
bestendiger / denn das heilige Euangelium.

So sprechen sie.
Die Concilia vnd Veter haben viel dinges geendert / aus dem heim-
lichen / freundlichen gesprech des heiligen Geistes / Nemlich / Das
die Priester nicht sollen Ehe- [H2v] weiber haben. Sihe da / Huren
mo[e]gen sie wol haben / Das hat jnen der heilige Geist in die ohren
geraunt / Sie mo[e]gen aber wol zusehen / das es nicht der leidige Teuffel
gewesen sey / Sintemal sie so offentlich vnd vnuerschempt handlen /
wider Gottes wort / vnd die heilige Go[e]ttliche schrifft.

Sie sagen.
Wo zween oder drey versamlet sind in meinem Namen / da bin ich
mitten vnter jnen. Das ist war / Sie sehen aber zu / das sie nicht ins
Teuffels namen versammlet sein / Das es nicht ein schwartzer Rabe sey

guild,[73] brotherhoods[74] and other such things that they have patched together.

Indeed, it is a crude, callous blindness, that they dare to say, write, and preach, that the pope and the prelates have power to change the gospel and God's Word. On that basis others might come over [a period of] forty or fifty years and do the same thing. What would be the final result? In such a case the teaching, statutes, and orders of the artisans, the cobbler and the tailor, would be more certain and reliable than the holy gospel.[75]

They speak in this manner:
The councils and fathers have changed many things on the basis of the secret, intimate conversation with the Holy Spirit, namely, that the priests should not have wives. Just look, they sure can have whores.[76] The Holy Spirit did whisper that in their ears. They had just better be sure that it was not the accursed devil since they so publicly and unashamedly act against God's Word and the Holy Scripture.

They say:
Where two or three are gathered in my name, there I am in their midst" [Matt. 18:20].[77] That is true. They should be sure, however, that they are not gathered in the name of the devil, that it is not a

---

73   The "calands" of the priests was a kind of brotherhood or association, which met on the first day (Calands) of each month for prayer, etc.

74   Brotherhoods were organizations formed for common prayer and devotional exercises. They also functioned as a kind of "life insurance" by paying for masses for the souls of deceased members and sometimes giving some financial support to their families.

75   A comparison of the church's teaching with the regulations that governed the conduct of trade in the guilds of the artisans.

76   The papal insistence on clerical celibacy was seen by Evangelicals as a tyrannous imposition upon priests and a denial of the goodness of God's good gift of marriage. Spangenberg is referring here also to the problem of priestly concubinage.

77   This is a reference to church councils, the authority of which Evangelicals placed at a lower level than did their Roman Catholic counterparts. At the Leipzig Debate in 1519 Luther contended against the Roman Catholic theologian John Eck that councils could err.

/ der vber jren Concilijs gemalet ist / Denn aus dem geschrey erkennet
man den Vogel / Vnd aus den fru[e]chten / die art des Baums.

[H3r] Weiter sagen sie.

Sie sitzen an der Apostel stat / derhalben mo[e]gen sie ordenen vnd
setzen / was sie gelu[e]stet. Wolan / so lasse sie zeugnis geben / das sie
aus dem heiligen Geist reden / wie die Aposteln. Sie sehen aber zu /
das sie nicht etwan an Hannas vnd Caiphas / oder an Judas stat sitzen
/ sintemal sie also offentlich vnd freuelich / wirder [!] Christum vnd
seine Lere handeln.

Das sie aber zu jrem behelff sagen / der Bapst ko[e]nne nicht jrren
/ mag wol sein / Denn die sieben oder acht Personen / die in vom
Pallatio jn Sanct Peters Mu[e]nster tragen / wissen freilich den weg
wol / Reitet er aber / so hat er abermals / die voran reiten / vnd den
weg auch wol wissen / das er freilich nicht jrren kan / er gehe oder
[H3v] reite. Vestehen [!] aber / als ko[e]nne der Bapst nicht jrren in
des Glaubens sachen / vnd meinen das mit ernst / So sind sie freilich
die gro[e]sten Heuchler / ja Lu[e]gener / so auff Erden komen sind
/ Denn wie solt der nicht jrren / der die heilige Schrifft / vnd Gottes
wort nicht zum Stabe vnd zur Lucernen hat / Da mus von not wegen
folgen eitel jrren / wancken vnd pampeln / stammeln vnd straucheln.
Vnd weil ein Blinder den andern fu[e]ret / mu[e]ssen endlich / beide
/ Lerer vnd Ju[e]nger / in die Hellische gruben fallen.

black raven[78] that is pictured above their councils. For from its cry you recognize the bird, and from its fruit you recognize what kind of tree it is [Matt. 7:17-20].

Further they say:
They sit in the place of the apostles, and because of that they may order and institute whatever they wish.[79] Wait a minute! Let them give witness that they speak from the Holy Spirit, as did the apostles. They should be careful that they are not sitting in the seats of Annas and Caiaphas [Luke 3:2],[80] or on Judas' seat [Luke 22:47-48] since they act so openly and cheerfully against Christ and his teaching.

They say in their defense that the pope cannot make a false turn.[81] That may well be. For the seven or eight people that carry him from the palace in Saint Peter's Basilica surely know the way well. If he rides [on a horse], he has those who ride ahead of him and know the way, so he indeed cannot make a false turn, whether he walks or rides. If understood, however, in the sense that the pope cannot make a false turn in matters of faith and they mean that seriously, they are indeed the greatest hypocrites and liars that have ever been on earth. How is it possible for someone not to make a false turn who does not take the Holy Scripture and the Word of God as a staff and lantern. The result must necessarily be nothing but error, swinging and swaying in all directions, stuttering and stumbling. And because one blind person must lead the other, finally both teachers and disciples fall into the ditch of hell [Matt. 15:14].

---

78   Black ravens were believed to be messengers from Satan in popular medieval belief.

79   A reference to the claim that bishops, and above all the Bishop of Rome, the pope, had authority granted to them by God as the vicars of Christ.

80   Annas and Caiaphas were successive high priests in Jerusalem at the time of Jesus Christ and thus leaders of the Jewish "council," the Sanhedrin. Both played a key role in his condemnation, cf. John 18:13-14, 24.

81   Spangenberg here makes a wordplay with the word "irren," which meant both to go astray and to err.

Es feilet den Papisten / vnd jren Gensepredigern vnd Lumpenweschern
nirgend an / denn das sie zu fru[e]he ausgeflogen sind / Sie wo[e]llen
der Schrifft meister sein / vnd haben sie noch nicht von ferns [H4r]
gegru[e]sset / Wollen bald gros gehalten / Licentiaten vnd Doctores
sein / vnd sind noch nie Phisicanten worden / Sie sind veraltet vnd
verschimmelt in der lausigen Papisterey / Scholasterey vnd Fabelwerck
/ in jren Heidnischen vnd Ju[e]dischen Ceremonien vnd Dockenwerck
/ das jnen nu schwerlich zu helffen ist / Denn das sie so steiff auff jrem
kopf stehen / ist ein lauter zagen / vnd wol halb ein verzweiffelung. Sie
dencken also / Ey du bist nu ein alter Papist / ein verdorbener Christ
/ wilt bleiben wie du bist / wirst doch nicht anders / Alte Hunde sind
bo[e]s bendig zu machen / Zeuchstu Schaffskleider an / so meldet dich
doch die stimme / das du ein Wolff bist / Vnd verrhaten dich doch die
Esels ohren / ob du schon ein Lewenhaut anthust. Es ist / Gott lob /
[H4v] mit den armen Leuten dahin komen / das sie nichts wissen /
auch nichts lernen / Vnd dasselbe / das sie gelernet haben / ko[e]nnen
sie nicht zu marckt bringen / werden stummer auff dem wercke / Strafft
man sie mit Gottes worte / vnd sagt jnen ins spiel / so lauffen sie zu jrer
Oberkeit / klagens weinend / wie die Kinder in der Schule / Du[e]rffen
dennoch rhu[e]men / sie haben zwey oder drey hundert gu[e]lden in
Hohen Schulen verzert / vnd verstudirt. Warlich / des rhu[e]mens
mo[e]chten sie wol stille schweigen / Denn / haben sie so viel verzeret
/ vnd nicht mehr kunst dauon bracht / denn sie noch an tag geben / so
ist zu fu[e]rchten / sie haben nicht in Codicibus / sondern in Calicibus
/ studirt / Nicht das Scribere / sondern das Bibere / geu[e]bt / Aber es
geschicht [H5r] jnen eitel recht / Sie wo[e]llen die liebe Warheit nicht

Nothing can make these papists and their goose-preachers[82] and rag-washers[83] responsible, for they have flown the nest too soon. They want to be the masters of Scripture, but they have not yet even waved at it from afar. They want to be regarded as important, they want to be *licentiates* and *doctores*,[84] and they have not yet attained the status of a peasant with folk wisdom.[85] They have become outdated, covered with mold in their lousy papism, scholasticism, and fables, in their heathen, Jewish ceremonies and children's games,[86] and so it is difficult to be of help to them. For the fact that they are so fiercely stubborn is due to their faint-heartedness. They are halfway in despair. They think, "Sure, you are an old papist, a corrupted Christian, and you want to remain the way you are. You will not change." You cannot teach old dogs new tricks. If you put on sheep's clothing, your voice still gives it away that you are a wolf. Your donkey-ears betray you even though you put on a lion skin. Praise God, it has come to the point with the poor people that they know nothing and learn nothing, and they cannot make any use of what they have learned. They are getting ever less responsible. If they are called to repentance with God's Word and are called to account, they run to the authorities and complain, with tears in their eyes, like schoolchildren, but they nevertheless can boast that they have invested two or three hundred Gulden[87] in the university and used them up in their studies. Indeed, they should just be silent with their boasting, for they have invested so much and have not gained any skill from it than they display until now, so it is to be feared that have not studied in *Codicibus* but in *Calcibus*,[88] they have not practiced writing but drinking. It serves them right. They do not want to have the precious truth, and so

---

82   A preacher who preaches without any thought to the effect of his preaching, or who preaches silliness.

83   A prattler or babbler.

84   Two medieval academic degrees.

85   "Physicus" was a term for someone, particularly among the peasants, who was knowledgeable in folk medicine and folklore.

86   "Dockenwerk" is a early modern high German expression for children's games or play.

87   A monetary unit of the time, worth about the price of a full-grown pig.

88   That is, they have not studied the books that contain theology but rather have learned to calculate how much money they have, a complaint against the mercenary demands for payment for ecclesiastical services.

haben / darumb mu[e]ssen sie sich auch jr lebenlang / mit eitel lu[e]gen
schleppen / Sie wo[e]llen Christum nicht zum Doctor vnd Hirten haben
/ So mu[e]ssen sie leiden / das der Antichrist / vnd der hellische Wolff
/ der Teuffel / vber sie hirschet. Gott behu[e]te alle frome Christliche
hertzen fur jrem Saurteig vund falscher lere / AMEN.

[H5v] Vom rechten Creutz der Christen
DAs hu[e]ltzern Creutz Christi hat Christus nicht heissen tragen /
da er sagt / Luce 9. Wer mir folgen will / der verleugne sich selbs / vnd
neme sein Creutz auff sich teglich / vnd folge Mir nach. Da ho[e]ret was
Christus saget / Er neme sein Creutz auff sich / sagt er / nicht mein.
Was vns Gott fur ein Creutz / leiden / tru[e]bsal vnd kranckheit aufflegt
/ das sollen wir Christo mit gedult nachtragen. Wie Christus durch
beru[e]rung seines aller reinesten fleischs in der Tauff / den Jordan / vnd
alle wasser / geheiliget hat / Also hat er auch durch beru[e]rung seines
allerheiligsten Fleisches vnd Bluts / alles leiden / armut / tru[e]bsal
/ ja den Tod selbs geheiliget / die Maledeiung ge- [H6r] benedeiet /
den Tod erwu[e]rget / vnd die su[e]nde vertilget. Christus sahe wol /
das wir fur dem Creutz vnd leiden wu[e]rden erschrecken / Darumb
wolt ers vns / als ein guter Hirte / vnd getrewer Artzt / su[e]s vnd
vnschedlich machen / Also / das man eines Christen tod nicht anders
solt ansehen / denn wie die Ehrne schlange Mosi / welche allenthalben
eine gestalt hette / wie ein rechte Schlange / vnd doch weder leben
noch gifft hette.

Christen sterben wol / wie ander Leute / komen auch in tod / aber
sie verbleiben nicht drinnen / sondern gehen den zeitlichen tod / ins
ewige Leben. Darzu helff vns Jhesus Christus vnser Heiland / Amen.

[H6v blank]

[H7r] Der CXIIII. Psalm
in Gebetsweise.

O Gott / Du hast dein Volck Jsrael wunderbarlich vnd gewaltiglich
aus Egyptenland gefu[e]ret / Lieber HErr / thue vns auch nach deiner
gu[e]te vnd trewe / Das alle Ehre allein deinem Namen bleibe / vnd
nicht vns / in allem dem / das du vns guts thust / Sey vnser hu[e]lffe
vnd schutz ewiglich / Segene vns / vnd lasse vns deine gesegneten sein
/ So wollen wir dich ewiglich loben / Amen.

they must drag themselves around their whole life long with lies. They do not want to have Christ as their teacher and shepherd, so they have to suffer it that the Antichrist and the wolf from hell, the devil, lord it over them. May God protect all pious Christian hearts from this leaven and false teaching. Amen.

On the True Cross of the Christians
Christ was not referring to carrying his own wooden cross when he said in Luke 9 [:23], "Whoever wants to follow me must deny himself, and take up his cross each day and follow me." Listen to what Christ says: "he should take up his cross," he said, not "my cross." We should bear whatever kind of cross God lays upon us, suffering, tribulation, and sickness, for Christ with patience. As Christ sanctified the Jordan and all water by touching it with his most pure flesh in baptism [Matt. 3:13-17], so he also sanctified all suffering, poverty, tribulation, yes even death itself, by touching it with his most holy flesh and blood. He blessed the curse, he strangled death, and he destroyed sin. Christ indeed saw that we would have great fear in the face of the cross and suffering. Therefore, as a good shepherd and a faithful physician, he wanted to make this suffering pleasant and innocuous for us, so that the death of a Christian should be viewed in no other way than as the iron serpent of Moses, which in every respect had a form like a real snake, but which was not alive and had no poison [Num. 21:8-9].

Certainly, Christians die like other people. The enter death, but they do not remain there but rather exchange temporal death for eternal life. May Jesus Christ our Savior help us to attain this. Amen.

Psalm 114
in the form of a prayer

O God, you have led your people Israel out of Egypt in a miraculous and powerful way. Dear Lord, act toward us according to your goodness and faithfulness, that all glory may remain alone for your name, and not for us, in all that you have done good for us. Be our help and protection forever. Bless us, and let us be among the ones you bless. We want to praise you forever. Amen.

[H7v] Gedruckt zu
Wittemberg:
durch Georgen
Rhaw.

Printed at
Wittenberg,
by Georg
Rhau.

.

INDEX OF BIBLICAL CITATIONS

INDEX OF NAMES AND PLACES

INDEX OF SUBJECTS